Ashley's Story

Michael R. Knetzger, Author

M. Louise Damiano, Editor

Jeremy Muraski, Cover Design

DEDICATION

First and foremost, this book is dedicated to Ashley. May your contagious personality, sense of humor, and love of others continue to make a difference from above.

This book is also dedicated to Ashley's mother, Lisa; her sister, Madeline; and her brother, Noah. Although Ashley's death has left scars, you continue to be driven to serve and change lives.

To all the brave men and women who choose to wear the uniform and protect and serve people across America, THANK YOU! Never forget that you do make a difference in the lives of others.

A portion of the proceeds received for this book support the *Ashley Knetzger Scholarship* at the Northeast Wisconsin Technical College (NWTC) Foundation. Ashley's scholarship is awarded each year to a student entering the nursing profession.

ABOUT THE AUTHOR

Mike Knetzger is in his 23rd year of service as a police officer with the Green Bay Police Department (GBPD), currently assigned to the Power Shift. Mr. Knetzger is also a member of the SWAT team and Training Unit. In addition, Mr. Knetzger is a certified Department of Justice and Wisconsin Technical College System instructor and has been teaching part-time for the past 16 years at Northeast Wisconsin Technical College (NWTC). Mr. Knetzger teaches in the criminal justice program, police academy, and specialized law enforcement topics. Mr. Knetzger is also affiliated with criminal justice programs at CTU*online* and Rasmussen College. Mr. Knetzger is a Subject Matter Expert (SME) for Pearson Education and has authored three other books, "Investigating High-Tech Crime," "True Crime in Titletown, USA ~ Cold Cases," and "Careers in Public Safety: Cop or Correctional Officer?" In memory of his 18-year-old step-daughter, Ashley, Mr. Knetzger is an advocate for stronger drunk driving laws in Wisconsin and social change.

Mr. Knetzger has shared *Ashley's Story* to law enforcement groups, high school and college students, all branches of the U.S. Armed Forces and community groups. To schedule Mr. Knetzger for a presentation or keynote for your organization, contact him directly through Ashley's website: WWW.ASHLEYSTORY.ORG.

ACKNOWLEDGEMENTS

The overwhelming support that we received after Ashley's death makes it impossible to mention every person who made a difference during our most difficult moments. THANK YOU seems to fall short of the gratitude so many deserve. At the same time, some organizations and individuals have played a unique role in supporting our efforts to make a difference in Ashley's memory. You may not be mentioned in *Ashley's Story*, but you're not forgotten.

Texas Roadhouse restaurant, where Ashley worked, provides gift certificates in support of the annual Ashley Knetzger OWI Award. Ashley's other employer, Red Robin restaurant, made a gracious financial donation to our family days after her death. Dave Labar at Ashwaubenon Bowling Alley hosted a fundraiser for the Ashley Knetzger scholarship fund and helped raise thousands to support students entering the nursing profession at NWTC. We are forever thankful for your generosity.

All of the brave men and women of the Ashwaubenon Public Safety Department, Brown County Sheriff's Department, DePere Police Department, Green Bay Police Department, Oneida Police Department, and Hobart-Lawrence Police Department comprise the Brown County OWI Task Force and continue to take drunk drivers off the streets before they have the chance to seriously injure or kill others. To all the officers who worked my shifts while we healed, THANK YOU. The time you took away from your family helped my family heal.

Sarah Thomsen, you are one of the best reporters in the business. Thank you for your compassion and empathy that you bring to each news story, especially when working with crime victims.

INTRODUCTION

You might be reading this book because you're a burned out cop looking for a way to refuel and find your lost motivation. You might be a student seeking inspiration or confirmation of your career choice. You might be a teen living in a home where your parent(s) is a substance abuser and you have trouble seeing hope for the future. You may be a parent who has suffered the tragic and sudden death of a child and are seeking understanding-- something or somebody you can relate to. You might be a step-parent who, without question, accepted, loved, raised, and became that genuine parent in a step-child's life. Maybe you just enjoy a good cop story.

Whoever you are, this book was written for you. It's a book about my path through life that may help you find yours. It's a book about turning tragedy into triumph and doing what you can to make a difference. It's a book about anger, sadness, and healing. It's a true story that can change lives.

This book is written from the heart with no punches pulled. It must be this way to make the most impact. This story is also told from my perspective and recollection of the tragic events surrounding it. Parts of the story and names are intentionally omitted to protect identity and reputation. Some parts of it will never be told. This story is about life, death, and living again.

Ashley's Story is about her life and death, and how she affected me, her step-dad. A step-dad can become the "dad" who makes a difference in a child's life. Sometimes, the step-dad becomes the only "dad" a child has. From the moment I met Ashley, I never thought twice about raising her. A new relationship that includes a child is not always successful, especially if the outsider, the new boyfriend, doesn't want to have children or doesn't feel comfortable interacting with or raising a child. This was never a thought when I met Ashley's mom, Lisa. In fact, my affection for Ashley was yet another reason to marry Lisa. Ashley allowed me to fulfill a promise I made to myself earlier in life, to be the best dad and positive influence in my child's life. Ashley allowed me to carry out that promise. I never considered Ashley my step-daughter, but rather my daughter. A few years into our marriage, Ashley paid me a great compliment when she came home from school one day. She showed us some of her school work and at the top right corner she had written "Ashley Knetzger." I never demanded or even suggested that Ashley take my last name; she did this on her own. I was touched. It made me realize the power of positive influence. From that day forth, she was always "Ashley Knetzger." During her early teenage years, Ashley often expressed her desire to legally change her last name. When she was 16 years old, at her request, we contacted an attorney and inquired about a name change. We discovered that it would be easiest for Ashley to change her last name on her own when she turned 18, when the request would be honored without contest. Just prior to her death, we had obtained all of the necessary papers for her to change her last name to Knetzger. Unfortunately, that never happened. We carried out Ashley's wishes by inscribing her headstone with the name "Ashley Knetzger."

For all step-dads out there who love a step-son or daughter as your own – trust me – you do make a difference in their lives. This book is for you too.

Police officers, this book is also written for you. When you became a police officer, you believed that you could make a difference; at least that's what you told the oral interview board before you were hired. You must have been convincing, because you earned the privilege to wear the uniform, took an oath, and were given the opportunity to act on your convictions. Unfortunately, police work has the potential to cause good people to question themselves, and in a few years you may have lost that drive to make a difference and have seen the worst of humanity over and over again. This can easily cause you to lose sight of why you put the uniform on the first time. I get it, because I've been there. *Ashley's Story* is also about how police officers can and do make a difference in the lives of others. I have seen and experienced the difference that police officers can make. Society also demands and expects you to make a difference and be able to handle everything thrown at you, from dangerous, weapons-related calls to emotionally charged death notifications. One moment you may be taking a dangerous armed robbery suspect in custody, and the next delivering news to next-of-kin that their loved one is dead. The way a death notification is made does make a difference in long-term recovery and is another important part of *Ashley's Story*.

Ashley's Story also gives insight into the unpredictable world of police work. One moment an officer can be relaxed but alert, and the next moment exposed to a rush of adrenaline while handling a dangerous incident. Interactions with people can be sad, tragic, frightening, and even happy-- but always meaningful. The significance of an interaction depends upon one's perspective. The police officer may view it one way, while a crime victim or suspect will view it another. In a moment's notice, a police officer's day *and* life can change. After reading this book, your perspective may change. One moment you will be reading about Ashley and the next you will be reading about a call for service experienced by me. Enjoy the "ride-along"!

Ashley's Story may help rejuvenate and motivate you to go out and make a difference. By doing so, you bring honor to Ashley and the thousands of other crime victims in America each year. You – the brave men and women in uniform – fight for victims and ensure justice. Without you, nobody would.

Mike Knetzger, January 2016

Chapter I

COPS AREN'T BORN, THEY'RE MADE

I am a husband, dad, teacher, writer, and police officer. I was born and raised in Wisconsin--one of the worst drunk driving states in the nation. Not only does Wisconsin often lead the nation in drunk driving, it's also home to some of the highest rates of alcoholism and binge drinking. Although I was born in Milwaukee, I spent most of my childhood growing up in New Berlin, a bedroom community of about 35,000 just west of Milwaukee. My childhood was anything but normal, especially from the age of ten through 17. Unfortunately, very few of my childhood memories are positive.

On the outside, our home fit in well with the neighborhood, but the appearance was misleading. Behind closed doors, the insidious disease of alcoholism slowly tore the fabric of our family apart. I quickly learned how to avoid it. I saw alcohol as the devil. It was the cunning and crafty evil that I fled from each day. The idea of responsible alcohol consumption was a foreign concept. I spent most of my time wandering the streets and avoiding home. Merely existing in school was a struggle. Failing grades and dropping out of high school sports was the result. "Why me?" was a frequent thought as I struggled to figure out this challenging game called "life."

It was fair to consider me a lost teen. It was the 1980s and I had no idea what I wanted to do with my life. I quickly learned from a counselor that the alcoholic won't get better until they admit that they have a problem. Too often the problem isn't realized until they hit rock bottom. I will never forget that defining moment. He had exited his car with a glass liquor bottle in hand. After parking in our driveway, he fell, his head smashing into the bottle. He was taken to a local hospital where I visited him later that night. I stopped a few feet from his hospital bed and looked at him: On his back, pale, weak, and looking barely alive. His thin, 5'7" frame looked defeated, alcoholism having taken its toll. I didn't know what to think, but sadness overcame me. He extended his right hand toward me. I slowly walked to him. His gray eyes looked like they had sunken in his skull. He grabbed my left hand and said the words that I had been longing to hear: "Son, I have a problem."

It is well known that alcoholics will never get the help they need until they admit they have a problem. This was that defining moment, and he got help. He got better! I'm happy to report that dad has been sober for over 20 years!

Within days after dad admitted that he had a problem, for the first time I had some hope for the future. I was 17 years old and sitting on the trunk of my parents' car. I had taken up smoking cigarettes and lit up. The cigarettes matched my "troubled" appearance. I was 5'6" with a build my mom described as "husky" and brown, shoulder-length hair. My appearance fit in well with the 1980s "hard rock" look.

It was a clear night and I stared at the stars. I made a commitment to myself that I would not do to my family what alcoholism had done to ours. I also thought about making a difference in the lives of others by becoming a police officer like my neighbor, Captain Terry Martorano, who lived across the street. I had seen him leave for work in his brown Waukesha County Sheriff's Department uniform over the years and this intrigued me.

Captain Martorano – or Terry, as I called him – was experienced and well respected. Like most people, he stood a good four inches taller than I. His salt-and-pepper hair showed his age and complemented his experienced look. Now in his mid-40s, Terry had worked his way through the ranks and served in patrol and drug investigations. Terry was also a Vietnam veteran and had the external scars to prove it. He never talked to me about it, but I imagined what he faced in police work each day was nothing like the jungle battlefield. Terry's voice commanded attention and his laugh was contagious.

I soon asked him if I could go on a ride-along and expressed my interest in police work. He set it up for me and within a month or two I was sitting in the passenger seat of a Waukesha County Sheriff's Department squad car on my first ride-along. It was spring 1990.

The night shift lasted from 11:00 p.m. to 7:00 a.m. I was somewhat nervous and had no idea what to expect. I was allowed to attend roll call and all of the deputies gave me an inquisitive look as if to say, "Who the hell is this kid?"

I was assigned to Deputy Bob Doffek, who looked less than thrilled with the assignment. After roll call, we walked out to his squad car and I initially just stood along the passenger side, unsure of what to do next.

"Sit down, kid!" barked Deputy Doffek. I nearly did, right on the pavement. He unlocked the front passenger side door and I slowly sat down being careful not to touch anything. The siren and light controls, mobile data terminal, radar unit, and microphone were directly to my left. The shotgun was mounted on a rack above my head.

It didn't take long for me to realize why marines are never ex-marines, but merely former marines. Deputy Doffek was prim and proper. His uniform was so crisp that I swore he must iron it before work and then again during his dinner break. His buzz cut followed him from his days in the marines along with his thin moustache. He stood a few inches above me, but much more slim and trim, with a ballistic vest wrapped tight around his torso. He clearly had "command presence" and a swagger of confidence when he walked. When he entered a room it was clear that he was confidently in control.

Deputy Doffek cracked his driver's side window just a bit, lit a "Winston" cigarette, took a drag, and exhaled the smoke out the window. He took a deep breath and then made his opinion of ride-alongs obvious. In a clear, loud tone he said, "I don't like ride-alongs, but I'm doing this as a favor for your neighbor. Just ask good questions." I replied, "Yes, sir" and wondered if I should just climb in the back seat, behind the cage where the prisoners go. My appearance was just the opposite of Deputy Doffek's: I looked like I should be driven to jail, behind the cage and not in front of it. During our dinner break that night, Deputy Doffek told the waitress, "Get this kid what he wants-- it's his last day of freedom." I'm pretty sure she believed him.

I had no idea what to expect during this night shift. Like many naïve teens, my perspectives where shaped by reality TV. COPS had only been airing for a few years and I was intrigued by the exciting, adrenaline-spiking parts of the job. The car chases, foot pursuits, and response to crimes in progress. That's what police work was all about—or so I thought.

Deputy Doffek was assigned to a traffic car on busy Interstate 94 (I-94) that ran all the way through Waukesha County, from the west end to the east, into the Milwaukee County. He was firm--very firm--but fair. Early in the night, we made a couple of traffic stops and they were always for 15 or more miles over the posted limit. As Deputy Doffek put it, "If you're doing 15 over, you know you are speeding." It was an idea that resonated and stuck with me. Most of the violators were cooperative and apologetic. One, however, wasn't.

It was shortly after midnight and we stopped a 21-year-old for speeding, 75 MPH in a 55 MPH zone. With his flashlight in his left hand and his weapon hand free, Deputy Doffek confidently, yet cautiously, walked up along the driver's side of this typical four-door sedan. I stood along the back passenger side of the vehicle, near the trunk. I could easily hear Deputy Doffek's commanding tone over the passing cars.

"I'm stopping you for speeding. License, please." I couldn't hear the driver's response, but he didn't comply with the request.

"Give me your license!" Deputy Doffek yelled. "I'm not going to ask you again!"

I flinched and started to reach into my back pocket, but quickly realized he wasn't yelling at *me*. The driver complied and was clearly told, "Stay in the car."

Deputy Doffek ran the man's name through teletype to check the driver's status and discovered no warrants for his arrest and a valid driver's license. "I want to give this kid the pink storm," exclaimed Deputy Doffek. What the heck is that, I wondered aloud. He explained, "It's when you issue multiple tickets to the same driver." The driver's copy was pink and apparently issuing several of them makes a point, like strong winds and rain do. In the end, this young man just got one pink ticket and was sent on his way.

We went back in service, squad 9203. It didn't take long for our first and last call of the night:

Dispatch: 9203
Deputy Doffek: Go ahead.
Dispatch: Respond to motorcycle crash, unknown injuries, Hwy 16 and JJ.
Deputy Doffek: 10-4, 10-76 (en-route)

8

With lights and sirens blaring, we headed to the crash scene. We were a good ten miles away, but we seemed to cover the distance in less than five minutes. When we arrived in the area, we checked the center median and shoulder of the road. It didn't take us long to find it. "There he is!" Deputy Doffek pointed out to his left, outside his driver's window, and quickly flipped a U-turn through the center median. His spotlight lit up a lifeless body that had been thrown at least fifty feet from a demolished crotch-rocket motorcycle. The man's body was abnormally contorted. Fractures were apparent; he may very well be dead. He had been going too fast, lost control, drove into the grassy median where the front tire dug into the soft turf, and the 21-year-old rider was thrown.

Deputy Doffek: Advise rescue, possible PNB (Pulseless, Non-Breather)
Dispatch: 10-4, they are 10-76 (en-route)
Deputy Doffek: Responding units, shut down the highway.

Within a few minutes the only vehicles on the highway were squad cars, an ambulance, and fire rigs. Deputy Doffek handed me at least ten road flares and instructed me to come with him. I followed and one hundred feet away from the victim we set up a rectangular pattern on the highway. Deputy Doffek explained the flares were for the Flight for Life rescue helicopter. "They're only sent when it's bad," he added.

Captain Terry also showed up. He didn't have much to do because the many experienced deputies had the situation well under control. The Captain was, however, tasked with making necessary arrangements to notify this man's family, potentially a dreaded death notification. I wondered what that terrible moment would be like, for the family that is awakened in the middle of the night and for the officers who must knock on their door. I didn't wish that pain on anyone. Little did I know this one defining moment was preparing me for the future.

The helicopter landed right in the middle of our flare pattern. EMTs and paramedics had been diligently working on the victim and doing everything they could to save his life. They quickly rolled the cot to the helicopter medics. It was a "load and go." In a matter of minutes, the chopper was headed to the nearest trauma center. Sadly, even the best medical care available couldn't save the young man's life.

We stayed at the scene until daylight. It would be the first time I would watch the sunrise from a highway. The sunlight helped the accident reconstructionist see the evidence needed to confirm what was already believed. The tire tracks were clearly seen leaving the highway, onto the gravel shoulder, and into the soft grass where a large divot was present, just behind the cycle that was still lying on its right side, mangled and destroyed. A high-speed, reckless and senseless fatal crash.

I guess Deputy Doffek liked me, even if it was just a little. "Call me Bob," he told me at the end of the shift. I would go on to ride along with Bob nearly 20 times over a two-year period. I'm forever thankful for the experiences and lessons learned during my ride alongs. They served to confirm my chosen occupation: a cop. It's what I wanted to be.

I brought a notebook with me and recorded my observations that night. I had no idea what questions to ask Deputy Doffek and surely didn't want to ask a stupid one or say the wrong thing. I choose my words carefully and quickly learned the wisdom of thinking before speaking. After all, whether we like it or not, people judge us by the words we use.

It was a busy night and I was immediately hooked. An office on wheels, outdoors, where your supervisor would leave you

10

alone and as long as you did your job. A self-directed job. A perfect fit for my personality! But my appearance didn't fit in. Within a week, I had the shoulder-length mullet cut off. I guess it was my first step into maturity, but first I needed to graduate from high school.

For the first time during high school, I actually felt motivated to do well. I knew I needed to graduate to even have the chance of getting into a technical college to study police science. Four-year colleges were out of the question. Well, I made it, with a whopping .19 grade point average – a D+. It wasn't the GPA of a rocket scientist; I wasn't voted most likely to succeed.

In fall of 1990, I enrolled as a full-time student in the police science program at Waukesha County Technical College (WCTC). I made it a personal mission to do well. While attending college, I also worked multiple part-time jobs in order to pay tuition. It's fair to say that I was hyper-motivated. I enjoyed most of my classes and like most students, I remembered both the exceptional instructors and the ones I couldn't stand. The average instructors were forgotten. One instructor, Tom McGuine, was particularly memorable.

Mr. McGuine was a retired LAPD homicide detective and he always reminded us how much experience he had: "21 years, six months, and three days." That is how long he worked for the LAPD. He saw and investigated more homicides in one year than I would likely see in my entire career. Although I never confirmed it, he was said to have been one of the detectives who worked the infamous "Hillside Strangler" case. The "Hillside Strangler" should have been referred to as "stranglers," because two killers, Angelo Buono and Kenneth Bianchi, were identified, arrested, and convicted of murdering at least 13 women in the hills above Los Angeles over a four-month period from late 1977 to 1978.

He was always formally addressed as Mr. McGuine. He had a wealth of knowledge and his presentation style captured my attention. Standing at least six feet, Mr. McGuine was well built, and his strong voice commanded respect. His dark hair was always above the collar and parted on the left. He cherished the power of silence. After asking the class a question, his brown eyes would stare over his wire rimmed glasses until he got a response. His weathered face remained still until he heard an answer. I'm sure it was the same approach he took in the interrogation room and I could only imagine how many confessions he had heard.

He also made it very clear that to do well in the class, students must read the textbook. Whining was also forbidden and writing frequently – either in a notebook or while completing research papers – was expected. He made the value of report writing known and those who didn't like writing, he quipped, "could always enroll in welding." Mr. McGuine was also not concerned about personal feelings and demanded excellence. He had a unique way of teaching and sometimes led to embarrassment.

Midway through the semester in Mr. McGuine's criminal investigations class, we were assigned our research paper topics. We could be assigned various topics: sexual assault investigations, property crimes investigations, and even homicide investigation. The last topic anyone wanted was homicide investigation. He could obviously pick that one apart. He knew too much. Well, you guessed it-- that was my topic.

I spent nearly eight hours researching, writing, and typing up the paper. The due date came and I confidently turned it in. A week later, Mr. McGuine returned the papers and although I earned an "A" on it, I made a crucial mistake. Mr. McGuine wanted to make me (and others) very aware of it.

"Knetzger, stand up!" My heart rate increased and I nervously obeyed Mr. McGuine's request. Twenty sets of eyes looked at me. I had no idea what was about to happen.

"Knetzger, please tell the class how you spelled homicide." I couldn't believe it! I felt like an idiot as I stared at the typewritten cover page. I took a deep breath and slowly said, "H-O-M-O-C-I-D-E." Some classmates chuckled while others remained silent. "Do you have a problem with certain segments of the population, Mr. Knetzger?" "No sir!" I replied and promptly sat down. How embarrassing! I couldn't believe that I had spelled homicide wrong! His point was made and the value of report writing was evident. It was a lesson – and a word – that I have never forgotten. His approach made me and many others better. His approach also helped others realize that law enforcement wasn't for them. It wasn't uncommon for his classes to begin with 30 students and finish with 20. If you couldn't handle Mr. McGuine's approach, then law enforcement wasn't for you.

Two years later, at 19 years old, I obtained my associate degree and graduated with high honors. This D+ high school student had found something that he was passionate about and continued to excel in criminal justice studies. I quickly discovered that you can be successful in anything as long as you are committed, passionate, and pour your heart-- and of course your mind-- into it.

I immediately enrolled myself in the police academy and six months later I was hired by the Town of Brookfield (WI) Police Department. While working full-time on the afternoon shift at the Brookfield Police Department, I continued my education and enrolled full-time on campus at Concordia University. My days consisted of four to five hours on campus in classrooms, followed by eight hour shifts at the police department. My determination and desire to succeed

13

kept me going and I graduated with honors, Summa Cum Laude, with a Bachelor of Science degree in justice and public policy. I would ultimately go on to earn a master's degree in public administration from the University of Wisconsin – Oshkosh.

To the high school students reading this book, I'm just one example of a below- average student who went on to have great success in college. The key is to find a course of study that you're truly passionate about and pour your heart into it. You will succeed.

Chapter II

THE NEW COP

The day had finally come: January 5, 1993, at the Town of Brookfield (WI) Town Hall to take my Oath of Office.

My heart was racing. I was excited, nervous, and eager. I was ready! I stood on one side of the police department front counter. The town clerk stood across from me and made it official. "Officer Knetzger, raise your right hand and repeat after me." I complied and took my first oath:

On my honor, I will never betray my badge, my integrity, my character, or the public trust. I will always have the courage to hold others accountable for our actions. I will always uphold the Constitution, and will remain loyal to my community and the agency that I serve.

"Congratulations," the town clerk said. We shook hands. I was a cop. 1860 was my number. I wasn't yet 21 and I was ready to make a difference!

Like most new officers, I went into the field for the first time feeling that I could change the world. I'm sure my Field Training Officer (FTO) chuckled at the motivated "young buck" that he was assigned to train. Maybe it helped remind him of the officer that he once was: clueless but with the right intentions. Well, it took only about six months to realize that a police officer cannot change the world. Nonetheless, an officer can change and affect the lives of others, some more so than others, one at a time. As I settled into my career I continued to believe that I was doing the right thing by taking a drunk driver off the road to save a life or arresting an abusive live-in boyfriend to spare the victim more abuse. I quickly learned about the "revolving door" of justice that tends to give criminals the opportunity to offend over and over again. The "first-time" drunk driver often becomes the second, third, or even tenth-time offender, which is not uncommon in Wisconsin. The domestic abuser is too often "forgiven" by the victim because she "loves" and can "change" him. Unfortunately, too many victims of domestic violence are caught in the "cycle of violence," a theory familiar to many police officers and one of the few "theories" that cops see played out again and again. For whatever reason, as cops we voluntarily expose ourselves to these conditions. We complain about the lack of justice and often want to give up because the courts always seem to set the arrested free the next day. I've heard "I wouldn't want your job" from many people.

Maybe our willingness to police fellow citizens and seek dangerous people in dangerous places makes us somewhat unstable, just like the man in the green jacket.

Dispatch: 1860
1860: Go ahead
Dispatch: Respond to the lobby of the cinema to check on the welfare of a man wearing a green jacket and mumbling to himself. Possible 10-96 (mentally ill subject).
1860: 10-4

Another unit was also dispatched to back me up and I arrived first. I walked up to the front doors of the cinema. The glare from the afternoon sun made it difficult to see inside. I opened the right side door and stepped into the vestibule. There he was. His odor. His clothing. His disheveled brown hair. Everything about this thin white man, in his 30's, about 5'08" tall, said, "I'm homeless."

He just stood and stared at me. I introduced myself, "Officer Knetzger, what's going on today?" He mumbled something in reply that I couldn't understand while he swayed slowly from

16

side-to-side. Something didn't seem right about this guy. His hands hung along the sides of his waist-length army green jacket.

I asked, "Do you have any weapons on you?" Again, he mumbled. His mannerisms convinced me that something was wrong. Was he armed? High on drugs? Mentally ill? I was caught in this vestibule, about the size of a large elevator, and I didn't have much room to move. I also couldn't let him into the theater and potentially risk the safety of other patrons. "Where is my cover?" I thought. I had to do something.

I told him, "Turn around and put your hands behind your back, I'm going to pat you down for weapons." He slowly turned away from me. His waist was in line with the heat register along the wall. Suddenly, his right hand reached into his coat pocket. At the same time, his wide eyes looked at me over his left shoulder. I feared, "He's going for a gun! He's going for a gun!"

I unsnapped and drew my Glock 10mm, took a step back, pointed it at him and yelled, "LET ME SEE YOUR HANDS!" He slowly turned towards me. My right index finger moved from alongside the frame to the trigger. I took a deep breath. I was just about to shoot. His blank stare looked right through me.

"A Walkman! Seriously, A Walkman!" He put his miniature cassette player on the heat register. He stood motionless, continuing to stare at me. I held him at gunpoint until my cover arrived. He was handcuffed and eventually taken to a mental health center.

It was the first time I nearly took a life.

Because of my childhood experiences, I perceived alcohol as pure evil. I hated everything about it. I despised it. As I

17

matured into adulthood and reached the magic age of 21, I enjoyed adult beverages now and then, but never on a regular basis. Even after a couple of beers, I would get extremely drowsy and sometimes have difficulty breathing. I soon discovered that I was allergic to beer, specifically the liquid yeast and hops. I guess this was a blessing in disguise. But as a police officer, I was exposed to alcohol and drugs from a different perspective. Most of the people I encountered in the field were under the influence of alcohol, drugs, or both. Nationwide, nearly 40 percent of police calls for service involve at least one person under the influence of alcohol and/or drugs (Bureau of Justice Statistics, 2010). During the nighttime hours, that percentage reaches 60 to 70 percent, depending upon the patrol area. I regularly saw the damage that alcoholism can cause a family and too often it reminded me of my own childhood. However, I used those experiences as motivation to make a difference by completing a thorough investigation and anything I could to make a charge "stick" against the intoxicated abuser or alcoholic in need of treatment. I also saw the damage, carnage, and death caused by drunk drivers. The injuries and death of innocent civilians in the path of a drunk driver at the wrong time disgusted me. I believe that homicide by intoxicated use is the number one preventable crime in America. It's simply prevented by making the choice to not drink and drive. It should never happen but all too often does. Since my career began in 1993, Wisconsin Department of Transportation records have documented over 4,000 alcohol related fatalities.

Although quickly frustrated by the bureaucracy of the criminal justice system, I soon realized that the only thing that mattered was how I *personally* did the job. I focused on what I could control; I adopted a personal strategy to conduct thorough investigations combined with reports so well written that the district attorney would have no choice but to charge the defendant. This approach also allowed me to go home at the end of each shift knowing that I did a job well.

Chapter III

THE PACKAGE DEAL

Wade Boggs, a former professional baseball player, once said, "Anyone can be a father, but it takes someone special to be a dad." I wanted to be someone special.

Cops, donuts, and coffee – a typical stereotype –has been confirmed by many cops who've been caught with powdered sugar on their uniform. All cops, especially the night shifters, have a favorite "cop shop" where they spend time enjoying free coffee and chatting with the night shift clerk. Not only is the coffee delicious (it always tastes better free!), it's also a way to engage the community, business owners and their employees. Sometimes this leads to an engagement of another sort!

I had my favorite stop, a 24-hour convenience store. The coffee and donuts were always the best price (free). I had conformed to the cop stereotype and consumed my share of those yummy round cakes or "power rings," as I call them. I would become a healthier cop a little later in life.

I was quickly attracted to the night shift clerk behind the counter. A cute, thin, short, 5'2", redhead. Her curly hair and button cheeks were occasionally brightened with a smile. Her name tag read LISA. She looked familiar, as though I had seen her before. I would soon learn that she was the same very attractive teenager who had worked at a local gas station in my hometown. I had often stopped there to fill up my red 1968 Chevy Chevelle. Being only sixteen or seventeen at the time myself, I hadn't had the courage to ask her out. Years later, I still lacked that courage!

Lisa was somewhat quiet but direct, and I liked that about her. She was not the prissy type. This brave police officer didn't

19

have the courage to ask her out or even for her phone number. For many nights and many months, I got to know Lisa a little better. I also found out that we had a mutual friend in a Brookfield firefighter and he became the match maker. He got her phone number for me.

The first phone call went well and when I asked her out, she said yes! We had planned a breakfast date after Lisa got off work in the morning-- or at least this is her recollection, which conflicts with mine. I don't recall even setting a "date" with her. I might have discussed having breakfast, but not an official date. Lisa claims I stood her up and never showed. I apologized and learned, "I'm sorry" and "Yes, dear," are valuable phrases that will preserve a marriage. Even though I apparently stood her up the first time, she agreed to another date. This one was official.

On February 7, 1994, we had our first date. We were both 22 years old, but Lisa was 17 days older. It is said that you will know – just simply know – when you meet the one you will marry. On that first date, I knew Lisa was the one. I immediately loved her brutal honesty. Lisa didn't pull any punches, and I found that refreshing. She wasn't fake, but she was tough. We had great conversation and had a lot in common. I also discovered that if I ever wanted to marry Lisa it was a package deal that included her four-year old daughter, Ashley. I never thought twice about it. Being a dad to Ashley could be the beginning of my promise from a few years earlier – to be a great dad and make a positive influence in a child's life.

A few days later, I visited Lisa at her apartment and met Ashley. This is a day I will never forget. Ashley's energy and happiness were contagious. Ashley stood a mere three feet, more than half of my "towering" 5'6." Her thick blonde hair extended past her shoulders. Her constant smile brightened her face as well as mine. She had faint freckles and bright blue eyes. She was not shy. I sat on the couch and she plopped on my lap. I was hooked! We all talked, laughed, and learned more about each other. The moment felt so right, like it was meant to be. From this moment on, I became "Mikey" and soon became the dad in Ashley's life.

I was committed to being the dad that all kids long for. I soon found myself spending days at Lisa's apartment taking care of Ashley while Lisa worked. I wasn't a gifted cook, but soon learned how to make macaroni and cheese, even *without* the directions! It was quite the accomplishment for me.

Going to Wal-Mart became a regular occurrence and I let Ashley wear whatever she wanted as long as it looked okay to me. Not the master of matching myself, I figured Ashley might know a bit more than I did. So when she wanted to wear a bright blue shirt, red sleeves, a pink vest, blue jeans, and rainbow colored socks, I was totally okay with that.

Ashley was extremely intelligent at a young age. She was well-spoken and cared about others. These are the same qualities important to the nursing profession, one she would eventually like to join. She loved her gray cat, Mr. Tisdale, but he didn't really like me – or anybody else - very much. The cat liked two people: Ashley and Lisa. I was the unwelcomed outsider. Mr. Tisdale and I reached a mutual agreement to leave each other alone.

Ashley's first nursing experience actually involved the affectionate Mr. Tisdale. I was helping Lisa move from her apartment when Mr. Tisdale decided to jump onto a glass mirror and shattered it. He cut a couple of his paws and bled all over. Lisa picked him up and the front of her light colored shirt quickly turned red. Frightened and rightfully concerned about the bleeding gray cat, Ashley did what all children would do, she called 911. The sadness and strain in her soft voice could be heard by the 911 operator on the other line.

"Please, send help, Mr. Tisdale is bleeding." At first, I didn't realize that Ashley had already activated the EMS system for Mr. Tisdale. I took over the phone call and the 911 operator began to chastise me about teaching children the responsible use of 911. I identified myself as a police officer and she changed her tone. I ended the call and turned our attention back to the bleeding cat. Ashley just wanted him to be okay and our veterinarian made sure of it.

Six months later, I made the commitment to marry Lisa and I wanted it to be a special moment. On a cop's salary, it took me some time to save the money for her ring. I was never able to save quite enough, so a credit card covered the rest. With the ring in hand, I took the three of us for a drive on a pleasant afternoon. We arrived at Whitnall Park, a popular southeastern Wisconsin hang out for teens. At nearly $1.00 per gallon for gas, it was an affordable teen destination. It was also the perfect setting for a marriage proposal.

As we wound through the park, I spotted the perfect tree. I can't tell you the type of tree. It had green leaves. It was about ten feet tall and it was surrounded by green grass. A few days earlier, I received permission from Lisa's dad to marry her. Now I just needed her to say yes!

 I led her by the hand and she knew something was up. My heart rate increased with each step toward the tree. I don't recall exactly what I said, but I tried to come up with something meaningful. While stumbling through my words, all I can remember hearing is, "Mikey, what are you doing? Mikey, what are you doing?" Ashley yelled from the parked car. I chuckled. As she grew up, so did her voice. Loud seemed to be Ashley's only volume setting.

I got down on one knee and after stumbling through my meaningful words that expressed my love for Lisa and Ashley, I asked, "Will you marry me?" I presumed she would say yes, but you just never know. "Yes!" exclaimed Lisa. "Thank God," I thought to myself as we embraced. Ashley's voice echoed in my head, "Mikey, what are you doing?" I replied silently to myself, "Ashley, I'm marrying your mom. And now I can officially be your dad."

I had found the love of my life. Now I would travel down a very different Lover's Lane.

Dispatch: 1860
1860: Go Ahead
Dispatch: City of Waukesha is in pursuit of a white Ford, 4 door, east bound I-94 approaching the town.

I was in the perfect position, on Barker Road at the Interstate 94 eastbound ramp and less than a minute later I saw them coming from behind me. The Ford flew by me, at least 90 miles-per-hour, being pursued by an unmarked black Crown Victoria – a drug unit – with flashing red and blue interior deck lights and a blaring siren. To ensure that the drug dealers knew that police were in fact chasing them and the unmarked drug unit was not just some misperceived rival drug dealer trying to stop and execute them, I had to become the primary unit.

It was about 9:30 p.m. and the light traffic allowed me to catch up rather quickly. As we entered the City of Brookfield and then quickly Milwaukee County, I was directly behind the drug dealers. My marked squad with red and blue flashing lights and siren made it very clear to them that the police were chasing them. Like many drug dealers fleeing police, they failed to stop and accelerated into Milwaukee County. My spotlight, shined directly into the passenger compartment, helped me see that there were four men inside the fleeing Ford, two in the front and two in the back. The two in the back seat – about 18 to 20 years old - continually looked back at me with desperation in their eyes. I must have had the same look, but my increased heart rate and adrenaline made for an exciting, yet dangerous moment.

I kept a safe distance, at least ten car lengths, but that wasn't nearly enough as we hit 100 miles per hour at times. The drug dealers weaved around the slower, innocent motorists. I stayed in the left lane and others eventually moved over. The Ford exited at Lovers Lane in the City of Milwaukee; as the drivers tried to drive through the "S" curves, it slid and rotated clockwise onto the center-median and rolled over. I couldn't believe it. The drug dealers went for one complete roll and the car landed back on its wheels.

1860: The vehicle crashed, start rescue
Dispatch: 10-4, advise nature of injuries
1860: 10-4, will advise

So many thoughts ran through my head. "Were they alive or dead?" "How badly injured?" "I sure hope I don't get jammed up for this!" "Should I have been chasing?" Even when armed drug dealers break the law, flee from police, and put many innocent lives in danger, the police are often accused of creating a hazard merely by chasing them. It seems illogical, but we must balance the risk to the general public with the necessity of chasing and immediately apprehending offenders. Under the stress of the moment and great personal risk, it can be difficult to apply this concept, but it is expected of us. When crashes happen, the necessity of the pursuit is often called into question. I knew I would have to justify this.

I couldn't believe my eyes! Either they were not injured or any injuries were very minor because all four of them ran and scattered into the bushes and shrubs that lined the streets. I couldn't decide whom to run after or if I should. I stood in disbelief for a few seconds. I couldn't identify the driver. With my gun drawn, I cautiously approached the white Ford.

1860: All occupants fled, in both directions.
Dispatch: 10-4, K-9 is 10-76

I peered through the passenger side front window and didn't see anybody else inside. I saw some blood on the steering wheel. On the back passenger side floor was a sobering reminder of the risks involved – a loaded 9mm black handgun. I was thankful I hadn't been fired upon.

A Waukesha drug agent joined me at the white Ford. "You believe that shit?" he asked. "It was supposed to be a buy-bust and they took off during the take down."

I asked, "Did you know they were armed?" He hadn't.

I learned later that the white Ford and the handgun were both stolen. I never found out if the suspects were ever apprehended. The K-9 unit was unable to locate them that night. I returned to the Town of Brookfield Police Department, wrote my report and explained my actions. I went home that night thinking about the irony that the chase and crash ended on Lovers Lane during the same week that I proposed to the love of my life.

Chapter IV

POLICING IN "TITLETOWN, USA"

After four years at the Brookfield Police Department, on January 5, 1997, I accepted a position with the Green Bay Police Department and moved to the "north woods." I wanted to work for a larger agency with other opportunities and a busier pace. I had applied for the West Allis Police Department and the Green Bay Police Department at the same time. Both agencies offered me a job the same week. After much consideration, we decided that "Titletown, USA" was the best choice. Green Bay was the larger city and home to the NFL's most storied franchise, The Green Bay Packers. Working the Packer home games was like having season tickets, but actually getting paid to watch them-- in between handling complaints of disorderly and intoxicated fans.

Being from the Milwaukee area, I had only been to Green Bay one other time, in 1996 to greet the Packer players at the airport when they arrived home after a playoff loss. Otherwise, besides the Packers, I knew little about Green Bay. Heck, I didn't even know people lived north of Green Bay. I soon realized that Green Bay was the biggest little city in the country and its football team was at the center of it. Without the Green Bay Packers, the City of Green Bay wouldn't be the same.

I successfully completed the 14-week field training program. I was already a cop but had to learn how to do things the "Green Bay way." I quickly found myself on my own and assigned to the afternoon shift. The city was busier than Brookfield. At times we had to make alternative arrangements for drunk drivers such as towing their car or getting them a ride rather than arresting them because other calls for service took priority. It was a manpower and attitude problem; some cops just didn't want to deal with drunk drivers because of the

26

average two-hour processing time and report writing that followed. It also took those officers off the road, forcing other officers to sometimes double their workload until the arresting officer was done with his drunk driving arrest.

I was assigned to the afternoon shift for my first three years with the GBPD. Things were going well at work, but not so much at home. Lisa and I had since had our second daughter, Madeline, and our son, Noah, was on the way. They were only 13 months apart. Working the afternoon shift was difficult on Lisa because she was essentially a single mom for half the day and sometimes all day. We were committed to never sending our kids to day care and that meant I had to work side jobs to support the five of us, including private Christian school tuition for Ashley and later for Madeline and Noah. There would be many days where I would work uniformed security at a local high school and then complete an eight and a half hour shift on the road. In addition, every third weekend I would spend working on and eventually finishing my Master's Degree in Public Administration at the University of Wisconsin – Oshkosh.

Needless to say, my constant absence quickly became old. It is often said in police work that if things are not going well at home, they won't go well at work. The constant demands and stresses of police work can quickly lead to burnout, a condition that changes once-driven police officers from wanting to change the world to bitter cops who call in sick with an "eye problem" because they can't "see" coming to work. Some officers realize their burnout moment and do what they can to change it. Others choose to live with it, which can lead to their demise. I was lucky and realized mine.

It was about 2:30 p.m. on a bright, warm, summer afternoon. We were busy and the lieutenant had given a quick roll call and ordered all 20 of us to get logged on ASAP. I selected the

Ford Crown Victoria closest to the back door, conducted a quick squad check, and got logged on.

As on most days, I drove out of the back parking lot toward my far east-side district. I slammed on my brakes and came to a stop. I looked to my left and anger consumed me. Right there, merely 20 feet away on the sidewalk, were four gang members-- two rivals on each side, squaring to fight. One had a baseball bat and the other a heavy gauge chain. They were just as surprised to see me as I was to see them. A good patrol officer would notify dispatch and get a cover officer rolling his way, but my burnout and frustration came to a boiling point at that moment.

I exited my squad and yelled, "What the hell are you doing?" They didn't reply. They didn't know if they should fight with each other, fight with me, stay, or run away. I ordered, "Drop your weapons!" They complied as the wooden bat and metal chain landed on the concrete. I told the rivals, "You two walk that way and you two walk the other way and get the hell out of here!" They quickly scattered. I picked up their weapons, threw them in my trunk, and drove away. "You idiot!" my internal voice screamed, "You could have been killed!"

This was a defining moment and I realized that something needed to change. I needed to get off this shift. A few months later I had the chance and went to the best shift on the agency: the power shift, working from 7:00 p.m. to 3:30 a.m. This new shift allowed me to actually eat dinner with my family each day, and what a difference time together at the dinner table can make!

I soon became a Field Training Officer (FTO) and it was rejuvenating to see new, energetic officers sitting next to me. They were the idealists, those who recently said during their oral interview that they wanted to make a difference in the community. Sometimes, so excited to work, they would say, "I can't believe they pay me for this." The veterans would be quick to tell them, "Don't worry, that won't last, but enjoy it while you can."

During my sixth year at the GBPD, I tested for and became a SWAT team member. It was another rejuvenating part of my career. It was something new, different, and challenging. I was proud to be a part of the team. The nature of the work also fueled the adrenaline junkie in me. It was dangerous, but I loved it!

In August 2004, Ashley entered high school at Fox Valley Lutheran High School in Appleton, WI. Throughout her high school years she alternated from wanting to be a doctor, lawyer, or teacher, but eventually settled on nursing. Every profession she considered was about helping people in some way or another. Her personality lent itself well to that. She didn't like the high school "cliques" and befriended many, from the nerds to the jocks. Often she was the one other students leaned on during difficult times. Ashley was a great listener and willing to stick up for others. Ashley also relished her role as big sister to her brother, Noah, and sister, Madeline.

Ashley grew up watching me work multiple jobs. It's fair to say that I was a "workaholic," and this drive rubbed off on Ashley. During her senior year in high school, Ashley played on the tennis team, had enrolled in preparatory courses at Northeast Wisconsin Technical College (NWTC) and obtained her Certified Nursing Assistant (CNA) license. While completing her studies, she also worked part-time at two restaurants, at a coffee shop, and occasionally as a receptionist at a real estate office. Ashley was driven to be successful and I had no doubt she was well on her way to making a difference in the lives of others.

Chapter V

FALLING OFF THE TRACKS

Although my career was back on track, I still thought I needed to do more. After all, I had a Master's Degree, and a promotion seemed to be the next step. In January 2006, I tested for and became a lieutenant.

Reluctantly, my wife supported me, even knowing that I would end up back on the afternoon shift, the one I had left years prior to be home more with Lisa and the kids. I expressed my concern to the chief and the impact that it would have on my family. He assured me it would be only temporary. Little did I know that "temporary" can mean years--many years. I took the promotion and it didn't take long to remember what working on the afternoon shift was like. When I was at home, the kids were in school, and when I was at work, they would be at home. Sure, I was "promoted" at work, but I was "demoted" at home. I missed out on some of the most important moments of Ashley's life, her concerts and tennis matches. Noah, now in third grade, and Madeline, in fourth grade, were becoming involved in school activities as well. I was able to attend their concerts and other events occasionally, but I didn't want to miss *any*. Sometimes, just to see me for thirty minutes each day, Lisa would bring the kids to the police department and have dinner with me. Those would be the best times of my day, but Lisa was once again relegated to the role of a single parent.

The promotion also required me to step away from the SWAT team and field training, two roles I would soon miss. Being a supervisor was something new and a change from "chasing the radio," which I needed. I was also assigned a new permanent squad number, 281R. After a brief supervisor training period,

I was on my own, and it didn't take long for me to chase something else.

I was traveling north on North Webster Avenue from University Avenue and an ATL (Attempt to Locate) came across my computer screen. A teletype had been received from police in Indiana advising that a suspect involved in taking a runaway juvenile from their state was last known to be driving a silver Ford Focus with Indiana plates, heading north on I-43 from Manitowoc towards Green Bay. The 15-year-old victim had placed a phone call to her parents from a rest stop at the southern county line. The teletype implied that the runaway juvenile may have been taken against her will by a 17-year-old male.

The I-43 on ramp was just ahead of me and I parked my unmarked squad on the interstate at the first emergency turn-around in the center median, just east of North Webster Avenue. This position allowed me to see northbound traffic. Less than a minute later, the Ford Focus drove right past me. The matching Indiana license plates were on it. I saw a teenaged male driver and female passenger. The driver avoided any eye contact me with and looked straight ahead. I guess he figured if he didn't look at me then I wouldn't see him.

I accelerated quickly to 70 MPH to catch up to the Ford. I notified dispatch and my initial plan was to follow the Ford, wait for additional marked patrol units to join me, and then make a traffic stop.

The Ford exited at North Webster Avenue and stopped at the bottom of the ramp. The left directional flashed on and off as the Ford slowly turned. The Ford continued south on North Webster and while it was underneath the interstate overpass, it began to pull over. I didn't turn my lights on yet and figured he was just stopping on his own. He must have known the gig was up, I thought. I pushed my emergency lights button and the red and blue flashing strobes left no doubt that the police were behind them.

Instead of stopping, the Ford quickly accelerated. I activated my siren and they sped up, obviously trying to get away. I could feel my heart rate increase. The adrenaline of a pursuit was kicking in. I took a deep breath before I keyed my microphone and said, "281 Robert, I'm in pursuit, south on Webster."

The driver displayed his intent immediately – get away at all costs. Without even tapping the brakes, he drove right through the red light at Radisson Street. Thankfully, other vehicles stopped and prevented a collision. Police pursuits are adrenaline packed, but very dangerous, and I knew this all too well. I prayed he wouldn't crash into an innocent motorist. Because this was a potential felony abduction suspect, I continued to pursue.

The Ford entered a residential area and headed east on Eastman Avenue. The driver had no concern about the 25 mile per hour speed limit as he continued in excess of 60. As I slowed before each intersection to make sure it was clear, he blew right through them.

As we continued east, I looked in my rear view mirror and saw a marked squad join me. I wanted the marked squad to take over my lead position. That way the fleeing driver couldn't later claim he was being pursued by some unmarked person posing as a police officer. The marked squad, with POLICE written on it, made it clear that they were fleeing from law enforcement.

The Ford sped through the last stop sign before the road ends at Clement Street. The only way the suspect could go was left into an apartment complex or right onto Clement, which lead to Farlin Avenue. This was the only way to University Avenue, a busy main thoroughfare out of the city, and I wanted to prevent this. The risk of escape and potential injury to others would be too great.

"We got him now," I thought to myself. I radioed to the squad behind me to turn south and then east on Farlin Avenue, which would put them directly in the path of the Ford. Officer David Paral acknowledged my request and quickly turned right.

I continued after the Ford and, just as I thought, it turned right onto Clement Street, and another quick right onto Farlin Avenue. The suspect slammed on the gas pedal, almost like he was aiming at Officer Paral's oncoming squad. Officer Paral stopped in his lane, creating a partial road block. The suspect could either stop or go around him. I couldn't believe what happened next.

The Ford slammed head-on into Officer Paral's squad. I immediately thought the worst – serious injuries to Officer Paral, the victim, and the suspect. Steam bellowed from the damaged engines. I immediately requested a rescue squad.

Still in disbelief of what happened, I saw Officer Paral climb across the front seat of his squad, open the passenger side door, and help me take the suspect into custody. I couldn't believe that Officer Paral's thin, 6'02" frame, withstood that impact. The victim and suspect were also not injured. Car crash technology had saved lives on this day.

It was discovered that the runaway juvenile had gone willingly with the suspect, her boyfriend, and it was her parent's car that had been stolen. Thankfully, we got their daughter back unharmed, but the vehicle was a total loss. All the suspect had to do was stop and this would have ended differently. Instead, he now faced several serious felonies and potentially time in prison.

With the bars on my shoulders and the gold badge, I drove around and watched officers work. I would occasionally answer questions from other officers. I only had to respond to high-risk calls for service or complaints against officers. Those most common complaints were the least enjoyable and often were from citizens about an officer's perceived disrespect. Most complaints were resolved with counseling and coaching officers regarding communication skills. Sometimes, however, discipline was necessary and that was the last thing I wanted to do. I avoided the use of the word "discipline" and I always tried to create training moments to help others improve.

I quickly became tired of watching officers do the police work I truly enjoyed. I missed doing that work! I had always believed that life was too short to be miserable at work and the job was changing me for the worse. I was often crabby. I began to hate going into work. My negative attitude and regular absence also began to wear at my marriage. I rarely saw Lisa and too often missed the kids' after school activities. It was like patrol on the afternoon shift, all over again. I needed to make a change. My family needed me to make a change.

On Monday, October 29, 2007 at about 10:30 in the morning, 18 months after the promotion, I stood in the kitchen at the counter with a cup of coffee. All three kids were in school. Lisa was seated at the kitchen table. A warm ray of sunshine traveled through the kitchen window and onto my feet. I was about to make the best decision of my career and, more importantly, for my family.

"Hey," I said to Lisa. "I'm miserable at work and I want to go back to patrol."

Honestly and straightforwardly, Lisa replied, "Good, because you have been a miserable person." Her honesty confirmed what I already knew. I wished she had told me sooner. She probably did, but I had failed to listen. Now it was time to make a change: go back to being a patrol officer or find work with another department.

I had begun looking for other employment, but really didn't want to start over again at another agency, not at 35 years old. I told the Chief of Police of my intentions. He did everything to convince me to stay a lieutenant, but couldn't address the underlying concern, my desire to do police work again. I approached the police union and asked if I could return to patrol. They were willing, but didn't know where my seniority would stand. Would I have to start at the bottom or could I return to my position of seniority at the time I had left? In the 150-year history of the police department, no one had requested a voluntarily demotion. After many discussions and a union vote, I was accepted back into the union at my position in seniority at the time I had left. I lost eleven seniority spots, but it was better than starting over at the bottom. Luckily, I also found myself back on the power shift. I was assigned back to my same zone, 362E, on the city's east side. Days later, I also was back on the SWAT team. March of 2008 marked the beginning of my career – again.

I did my best to begin repairing things at home. I was able to be more involved, spend more time with Lisa and the kids, and actually be present again. I had felt like an absent dad at times…it was nice to be back, but it didn't take long to tangle with some "real" K9's.

Dispatch: 362E
362E: Go ahead
Dispatch: Respond to 834 Abrams Street, anonymous tip that Jose Rodriguez is there, and has a felony 99 (warrant) for his arrest.
362E: 10-4

Two other units were dispatched with me. I was familiar with Jose. I had arrested him before, and the last time he fought with police. Jose was easy to spot. He had a tribal tattoo on his face that partially curved around his left eye, like a black half-moon. Jose was also short, about 5'5" tall and thin, maybe 140 pounds. Although his physique didn't intimidate, he had the "nobody can hurt me" attitude of the typical 20 year old.

I knocked on the front door of the side-by-side duplex. A female answered. It was Jose's girlfriend and this was her place. She stepped outside to talk to me and denied that Jose was here. Her denial was not very convincing and it was apparent that she was either trying to protect Jose or afraid to cooperate with police because she feared what he might do to her. I had her walk with me to the adjoining driveway. After our discussion, she gave us permission to enter her residence and arrest him on the warrant.

I requested a K-9 unit. Officer Mulrine and his K-9 partner, Lobo, arrived a few minutes later. Lobo, or "Loco" (Spanish for "crazy") as I called him, was very "energetic" and just simply wanted to find someone to bite. More than one officer had been bitten by Lobo. My anxiety was always a bit higher when Lobo was around, and I'm sure he could detect it.

"Green Bay Police K-9 Unit! Jose, we know you are in here, come out with your hands up or we will send the dog. You will get bitten." This necessary announcement was given a few times. Jose never showed himself. With guns drawn, four of us began to clear and search this two-bedroom, one-story duplex. No one was found on the first floor and only the basement needed to be cleared. I opened the basement door and Lobo was the first down the stairs. Lobo quickly ran completely around the very clean basement, up the stairs right at me, and then out the front door.

I heard Officer Mulrine yell after Lobo. I chuckled to myself as I walked down to the basement to do a quick secondary search. I was surprised by how clean it was. There was absolutely nothing on the basement floor. There was a residential washer and dryer along the north wall. I had checked inside washers and dryers many times in my career looking for lost or missing kids. Sometimes kids would fall asleep in them during a serious game of hide-and-seek. I never expected to find an adult in them!

As I opened the dryer door I was surprised to see the left side of Jose's face and tattoo. Jose had contorted himself inside. I slammed the door shut and announced, "I got him! He's in here." I kept the door pinned shut with my left hand, stood off to the right, and kept my handgun in my right hand, along my right leg. Two other officers came to my aid and got set. One had a bean bag shot gun. Another had an electronic weapon. We gave each other a nod. I opened the dryer door and orders were barked at Jose. "Get out and get on the ground!"

Little did I know that Lobo had returned. He ran down the stairs toward our voices and directly at me. It was nice to have him there too and I was sure that Jose would be bitten, especially if he started fighting. Lobo ran right past the open dryer. Jose's arms were extended out and he didn't have any weapons in his open hands. He appeared to be surrendering. Lobo then sniffed my left foot and shin.

I screamed in searing pain as Lobo bit my left shin. His teeth gripped on and above my high-top black boots. It wasn't the

37

initial bite that hurt, but the excruciating and crushing pressure that I felt as his jaws compressed. The barrel of my gun pointed at Lobo's head. I had no intention of shooting him, but I would be lying if I said it wasn't a thought. My left shin and foot went numb. At the same time, all I heard was Jose yelling, "I'm sorry, I'm sorry!" He later asked one of the other officers, "Can you let that officer know that I'm sorry he got bitten?" I'm not sure if Jose was truly sorry that I had been bitten or was just thankful he hadn't been Lobo's target.

Officer Mulrine grabbed Lobo by the back of the neck to control his head and get him off me. Lobo released, but then turned and bit Officer Mulrine on the right knee. "What the hell is wrong with that dog?" I thought to myself as I limped toward the stairs. I couldn't put weight on my left foot. Officers handcuffed and escorted Jose upstairs. I never saw him again.

I sat at the bottom of the stairs for a few minutes. As the numbness went away, it gave way to pain. I knew I had to get "cleared" at the hospital. I rolled up my pant leg to check on the injury, not sure what to expect. My boot side-zipper was crushed and I couldn't move it down. Blood dripped from a puncture wound just above my boot. I hobbled to my squad. "Knetzger, you want a rescue squad?" I turned down the offer, as my right leg was just fine. I drove to the hospital and limped inside.

Word had already spread that we were coming and what had happened. Nurses, like cops, have a demented sense of humor and they greeted me with "biting" wit.

Officer Mulrine joined me in the room and lay on the adjoining bed. "What the heck is wrong with your dog?" I asked. I expected to hear some rational explanation that only a K-9 handler could give.

Instead, Officer Mulrine replied, "I don't know, he got confused." Lobo seemed pretty certain to me when he was latched onto my leg. "Welcome back to patrol," I thought to myself, but it was still better than being a lieutenant.

One of Lobo's teeth made a nice hole into my left shin. It was cleaned well and luckily I didn't need a stitch. Lobo's scar remains, in my mind and on my shin.

Chapter VI

THE DEATH MESSENGER

"I love life so much; I want to be 18 forever."
~Ashley, three weeks before her death

My return to patrol was great; while away I had learned a lot about chasing the too-often self-serving pursuit of "success." I returned to old form, trying to be as proactive as possible while chasing the radio – responding to calls for service. The same calls I used to complain about before I was promoted didn't seem so bad anymore. It felt good to once again be in a position to actually make a difference in the lives of others. When not on a call, I would seek out drunk drivers. I had no empathy for a drunk driver and considered driving while intoxicated a selfish act. Too often I saw the senseless tragedy and death that drunk driving can cause. Not only had I responded to serious injury and fatal drunk driving crashes, I was also given the task of making my share of death notifications, the worst assignment an officer can have.

During the first fifteen years of my law enforcement career, I had arrested nearly 500 drunk drivers. Sadly, they are not hard to find in Wisconsin, especially during the night time hours. I also had the unfortunate experience of making five death notifications. Honestly, if given the chance to go to a "shots fired" call or a death notification, I would much rather go to the weapons call. At weapons calls, most cops have a sense of control. At a death notification, just the opposite is true: we cannot control the response of others – often a mother or father – after they receive the news that their loved one is dead.

The reaction to a death notification can be very unpredictable. Few officers and supervisors are properly trained in how to make a death notification. They often learn as they go, some better than others. When making the notification, the officer must be prepared for anything, from violence to a medical emergency. For example, in one notification, I told a father that his son had killed himself. The alcoholic son had put 150 pounds of weights onto a bench press bar and lowered it onto his throat. He left a note behind indicating his intent. Upon telling his estranged father of his son's death, he grabbed me by my uniform shirt and pushed me into a wall while yelling, "No, you're lying." He began to cry and all I could come up with was an apology. In another instance, I informed a 25 year-old woman that her boyfriend had been killed in an auto crash while driving her car. She collapsed in my arms, sobbed, and her tears dripped off my badge. Again, I could only say how sorry I was.

All the death notifications I had made in my career were consistent: I would make the notification, get helping resources to the grieving person, answer as many questions as I could, and leave at the appropriate time. I had no idea what happened next. I was about to find out.

On Tuesday, June 3, 2008 at approximately 8:00 p.m., Ashley finished her restaurant shift and drove her silver Nissan to a nearby restaurant to meet her good friend, Talhia Heroux, also 18. Ashley had graduated high school with honors ten days earlier. She and Talhia, also a recent graduate, enjoyed hanging out.

 Ashley had matured into a beautiful young woman. Her blue eyes matched a clear sky. Her loud, boisterous personality always filled a room. We always knew when Ashley was home. She had grown up and was inches taller than me. Her long, brown hair was as thick and flowing as the first day I met her. Her smile puffed her cheeks and her faint

freckles, like times gone by, had faded some. She had a prominent forehead. Her hair pulled back always made it a perfect place for dad's kiss goodbye each day before I went into work. Hours earlier, before leaving the house, I had kissed her forehead and said, "I love you." Those were to be the last three words I would say to her.

Ashley rode in Talhia's dark blue four-door 1992 Buick Lesabre. It was a typical teenager's car; not the best, but it got around town. They drove to a park, not too far from the Texas Roadhouse that they both worked at, and hung out with friends for about an hour. "I have to get home and spend time with mom," Ashley likely thought to herself. Spending time with mom was important to Ashley. Although Ashley was extremely busy between work and school, she always found time to spend with mom, especially when I was at work. Not only were they mother and daughter, Ashley and Lisa were best friends.

Ashley and Talhia said good bye to friends and drove back toward Texas Roadhouse.

Talhia stopped for the red light on Willard drive at S. Oneida Street. The parking lot of Texas Roadhouse was less than 100 feet in front of them. It was a beautiful summer night-- not a cloud in the sky, temperatures in the '70s-- a perfect way to start their Wisconsin summer vacation.

Two hours earlier, Anrietta Geske, 46, had visited a local bar on Green Bay's west side. She had recently relocated to Green Bay from Texas to reestablish her life. Recently divorced, her prized possessions were her silver 2002 Porsche Boxster convertible and her Chihuahua, who often accompanied her inside a handbag.

Straight Jaegermeister liquor on ice was Anrietta's drink of choice. She appeared to have a good time at the bar. The

42

surveillance cameras inside showed her dancing and chatting with others. She even brought her dog along in her purse. At that moment, Anrietta didn't have a care in the world. Her emotions, logic and common sense were all clouded by alcohol and possibly by other drugs as well. Anrietta had told others in the bar that she was bipolar. If she had been taking common psychiatric drugs to treat this disorder, they wouldn't mix well with alcohol and cause further impairment.

Anrietta's night at the bar was not a long one. While drinking her short evening away, she consumed at least four Jaegermeisters in two hours. That would amount to a blood alcohol content (BAC) of about .103. She had bragged to others about owning a Porsche and offered to show it off to a man or two. There were no takers. She walked out the back of the bar and into the alley where her silver Porsche convertible awaited. She squeezed behind the wheel, started the powerful sports car, and put it into drive.

Anrietta took the long way home. With the top down, she also enjoyed the beautiful weather, the moonlight reflecting off the calm river waters. Any sense of calm would-soon be over. Anrietta crossed back over the river, and like a fan going to the world famous Lambeau Field, Anrietta went west on Lombardi Avenue and then south on S. Oneida Street. She cruised along the east side of Lambeau Field in the right lane and stopped at a red light. A smaller, blue sporty-looking vehicle stopped alongside Anrietta. It was driven by a 16-year old boy, Tyler, with his 15-year-old girlfriend, Elizabeth next to him. Both drivers made eye contact, the kind of look that says, "Let's race." Tyler's car had a modified exhaust system that sounds like an angry bee upon acceleration. The light turned green and both drivers pushed their gas pedals to the floor.

The cars raced toward Willard Drive. The light on S. Oneida had turned from green, to yellow, to red. Talhia and Ashley's light had turned green. It was now 9:28 p.m.

"The light's red!" screamed Elizabeth to Tyler. He slowed down. Elizabeth later testified, "I saw her coming out of the corner of my eye and just like flying by us really fast like I have never really seen a car go that fast on the road or any road in general past me...she (Anrietta) was very like set back in her car, and her hair was just like flying all over because...the top was down."

The speed limit was 30 miles per hour. Anrietta wasn't about to stop. Her impaired judgment had led to racing and would now lead to murder.

Like a bullet spiraling toward its target, the Porsche crossed the path of Ashley and Talhia. The silver "bullet" approached at 86 to 92 miles per hour. Anrietta sped through the red light and the front end of her Porsche pierced the driver's door of Talhia's Buick. Talhia was crushed and shoved onto Ashley. The violent impact collapsed Ashley's seat, crushing her onto the passenger side floor board. She died there and was initially unseen by those first on scene. Like a spear, the Porsche impaled itself into the center of the Buick.

The front and back ends of the Buick wrapped around and "slapped" both sides of the Porsche, like a perverse hug, and partially unwound itself into a contorted backward "C." Both vehicles – a combined weight of at least 4,000 pounds - were now conjoined and stuck together. From the point of impact to final rest, on a completely dry road, they

44

traveled together 126 feet. Two vehicles stuck together after a crash is a rare sight. It only happens when one vehicle is going considerably faster than the other. That was exactly the case. The calculated speed of Talhia's Buick was approximately 12 miles per hour. All Ashley and Talhia were trying to do was get back to Ashley's vehicle so she could return home and spend time with mom. They never made it.

911 Operator: "Brown County 911,"

Frantic female caller: "There is an accident, a severe accident..."

911 Operator: "Where?"

Frantic female caller: "Oneida...hm, Oneida and..."

911 Operator: "Ma'am, Oneida and where?

Frantic female caller: "Ah...ah, Willard."

911 Operator: "Okay, you're in Ashwaubenon, okay, does anybody need an ambulance there?"

Frantic female caller: "I need an ambulance right now!"

911 Operator: "Okay, Ma'am, how many vehicles?"

Frantic female caller: "Two."

911 Operator: "How many people are injured?"

Just seconds before Ashley and Talhia were murdered, off duty Green Bay Officer Tom Kraus was driving his 15-year-old daughter home from a softball game. They were driving north on S. Oneida Street, just south of Willard Drive. Officer

Kraus later recounted, "I saw what looked like an explosion. I came upon the scene. Stopped my truck and did what I could to help. I walked towards the passenger side of the Buick and only saw one person inside (Talhia). I stood alongside the driver of the Porsche, noticed she (Anrietta) was alive, and grabbed a phone from a female who was on it with 911."

Officer Kraus: "This is TK from the city, who is this?"

911 Operator: "Hi, this is Jenna. How many people are injured?"

Officer Kraus: "We have one that is trapped, I don't know if she is living or dead...we need extrication now! We have at least two injured, one possibly fatal."

911 Operator: "Okay, so possibly two. Do you know what type of injuries at all?"

Officer Kraus: "Again, one is trapped underneath the steering wheel, she is complaining of leg pain. The other one I can't even see...she's trapped."

911 Operator: "Okay, are they both in one vehicle?"

Officer Kraus: "No, no, she was T-boned."

911 Operator: "Okay, alright, I have them going... Ashwaubenon Police"

Officer Kraus: "Do you want me to stay on?"

911 Operator: "I want you to stay on. Are they in traffic?"

Officer Kraus: "Yea...all of northbound is blocked off."

911 Operator: "All of northbound is blocked off, okay."

Officer Kraus: "I don't know if there is more people (in the Buick) or not. The car is full."

911 Operator: "The car is full?"

Officer Kraus: "And it's crushed…They're trapped."

911 Operator: "I just let them know that one is trapped for sure and possibly two patients."

Officer Kraus: Raises his voice and says to another witness along the passenger side of Talhia's Buick, "Can you see anybody? Two females in there. Are they talking? They're moaning, they're moaning."

Did others hear signs of life from Ashley and Talhia at the scene? Or the process of death?

In less than one minute, the police and rescue personnel were dispatched to the scene. The first unit would arrive moments later. No matter how quickly they went, it was too late for Ashley and Talhia. They were dead.

Officer Kraus could see only Talhia inside the Buick. Ashley was buried in the debris along the passenger side. Officer Kraus had no idea that the daughter of a fellow officer had just been murdered. He held Anrietta's left hand and did his best to assure her that she would be okay. It's just what good people do when they are trying to help and reassure injured people, even murderers. Anrietta complained of leg pain. Both legs were trapped under the steering wheel and dash, crushed and broken. The impact was so massive that her left high-heel pierced the firewall of her Porsche. It remained there until the jury rendered their verdict months later.

The scene was pure chaos. The entire roadway, in all directions, needed to be shut down. The ambulance and fire trucks with extrication equipment were still on their way. "Jaws of Life" are typically used to save lives. In this case they were used to remove two who had died. Anrietta was treated and removed from her Porsche. Her Chihuahua was found in the wreckage, alive-- and would later be blamed by Anrietta for causing the crash.

On scene, responding officers also discovered a bag of prescription medications on the passenger seat floor of the Porsche. These medications were for bipolar disorder with a clear warning label that read, "Do not mix with alcohol."

It was about 10:00 p.m. when a message arrived on my in-car computer screen: *Check out the double fatal in Ashwaubenon.* I could have looked up the incident, but my shift was over in 30 minutes and I just wanted to get home. I was also stuck on call. I had just finished counseling a mother regarding her reaction to allegations that her four-year-old daughter and another five-year-old neighbor boy had sexual contact. The boy had apparently encouraged the girl to "pee outside" while they were playing "house" and he asked her to touch his "pee-pee." Mom had created a disturbance at this boy's house. Mom's hysterical reaction was enough to frighten the boy's wheelchair-ridden grandmother into a panic attack. An ambulance also responded and ensured that grandma would be okay. Mom fled before we arrived and we later tracked her down at her apartment. She admitted to "overreacting" and apologized for putting the "fun" back in dysFUNction. My shift was ending early this night. I had taken some vacation time off to get some sleep before teaching at 7:15 a.m. the next morning at the police academy. I glanced at the "double fatal" message, never looked the call up, and deleted it. I remember thinking that some family would soon be receiving some very bad news. Unknown to me, the message was foretelling the future.

48

To avoid getting sent to any more calls, I quickly cleared the juvenile call and logged off (10-42 in law enforcement parlay). I walked in the house at about 10:40 p.m. Ice cubes fell into the glass tumbler that would soon contain my post-shift brandy and coke, a little "relaxer" to take the edge off before going to bed. I sat on the living room couch, grabbed the remote, and took in the latest headlines.

Three knocks came at the front door. Stinky, our elderly basset hound, barked. "Ashley, you're so lazy," I thought to myself. She would often come home at this time after working one of her three jobs and hanging out with friends. If one of us were up, instead of using her key to unlock the deadbolt, she would knock, knowing that we would let her in.

I peered through the glass panel and I saw the shoulder patch of the Brown County Sheriff's Department. I unlocked the deadbolt and saw a uniformed deputy standing on the porch. "What did Ashley do now?" I thought to myself. Ashley only had two other "run-ins" with police. Nothing serious, just teenager stuff. "We'll get through this, I'll just go pick her up at the police department." At least that's what I thought.

Two years earlier, shortly after Ashley got her driver's license, she was stopped by the police at 2:00 a.m. in a popular downtown bar district. The officer called my cell phone that night and I didn't expect any favors. We had always told Ashley not to expect any preferential treatment because her dad was a police officer. The officer parked her car and the next day Ashley insisted she was "looking for a Starbucks" with her friend. We never believed her...but she always stuck to that story.

My right shoulder leaned against the door frame. I completely expected to see Ashley there, but she wasn't. Deputy Tim Johnson stood directly in front of me. I glanced to my left and saw another deputy, Scott VandeVoort, as he stood motionless in the background. I looked back at Deputy Johnson and the silence was about to be broken. His clean-shaven face seemed drawn and his shoulders lowered as he began to speak. "Hi Mike, is Ashley your daughter?" I knew, deep down inside, I just knew what he was going to say next. "She was involved in an accident..."

Deputy Johnson continued, but I interrupted. "Is she dead?"

He hung his head and replied, "Yes." The message on my in car computer came rushing back to me: *Check out the double fatal in Ashwaubenon.*

I walked outside onto the porch and closed the door behind me. I took a deep breath, slowly exhaled, and tried to compose myself. I don't recall the next words spoken, but I was now standing on the driveway. I phoned the police department and told the night shift captain, Todd Thomas, "Todd, my daughter, Ashley, was killed tonight by a drunk driver." I asked him to send Officer Dave Steffens, a good family friend, to respond and be with Madeline, now 11, and Noah, 10. I called Chad Ramos, another officer, at home. He knew Madeline because she babysat for his son. It seemed to take forever for them to arrive. I stood on the driveway and cried, trying to imagine how I was going to tell Lisa.

Stinky continued to bark and woke up Madeline. I didn't know it at that moment, but she had peered through her bedroom window that overlooked the driveway and later told me, "Dad, I knew Ashley was dead when I saw you standing on the driveway, crying with the deputies." Although I had yet to tell her, Madeline was really the next to know that Ashley was dead.

Weeks later, Madeline was in her upstairs bedroom with Noah and a friend; they were having a sleep over. I had gone down downstairs to get a glass of water and overheard Madeline talking, "...then my Dad was on the driveway with the police..." She was retelling the story. It broke my heart and I slowly walked back to bed. The next morning she told me, "Dad, it was exactly 12:14 a.m. when I saw you outside with the police. It was exactly 12:28 a.m. when you told me that Ashley had been killed." This was exactly three hours from the time of the crash. When up late, Madeline was reminded of Ashley's death at these exact times every night; it's amazing what kids remember. It's unfair that they have to live with these awful memories.

 I slowly walked inside and the deputies followed. Dave and Chad arrived minutes later. Dave sat on the couch with Madeline by his side. He held her close, his right arm around her shoulders. I thought it best to let Noah sleep. The walk up the stairs seemed like it took forever. Every step was in slow motion. I didn't want to get to the top of the carpeted stairs; our bedroom door was to my right. I slowly opened the door. The light from the hallway illuminated the room and highlighted Lisa. She slept peacefully, not knowing her nightmare was about to begin.

I nudged her left shoulder. "Honey, honey, wake up...Ashley's been involved in an accident." She quickly

51

awoke and began to follow me out of the bedroom. "Put some clothes on…we need to get to the hospital," I continued to walk out of the bedroom and she stayed behind to change. I didn't have the courage to tell Lisa right away that Ashley was dead. The entire time she was getting ready to go she believed that Ashley was alive. I regret not telling her immediately and creating the false belief that Ashley was alive.

I sat on the couch and waited for Lisa. Minutes later, I heard her coming down the stairs; all of our lives were about to change forever.

Lisa rounded the corner into the living room and immediately stopped. She saw the deputies, Chad, and Dave. She knew something was wrong, very wrong. I was blunt. I knew no other way to tell her. I clearly said, "Honey, Ashley is dead." She took two steps towards the stairs and collapsed onto her knees burying her face in her hands. She screamed, "No, No, not my baby. I wish it were me!" I didn't know what to do. I just sat on the couch next to Madeline for what seemed like an eternity. Madeline crying. Lisa crying. I was crying. The house was filled with wailing. I walked over to Lisa and just held her. What else could I do?

The officers, all of them, were speechless. Breaks in the wailing were filled with silence. Deputy Johnson told us that the medical examiner was waiting for us at the hospital. We had to view Ashley's body. I had made many death notifications before, but left before family members were tasked with viewing their deceased loved one. It was something that is often portrayed on television, but few must do in real life. It was now my turn, our turn, to "confirm" the identity or, in our case, view Ashley for the first time in death.

Suddenly I realized I didn't know where Lisa was. I had lost track of her and she was no longer in the house. I began to feel panicked and thought she had just walked away. I wondered if she was OK. Honestly, I feared I was going to lose my wife. I checked every room on the first floor, even Ashley's room, and couldn't find her. I even thought Lisa might walk into the wooded area behind our house and kill herself. Lisa and Ashley would often take walks in the woods along the East River. Logically, I thought, that is where she would go-- a place where they had spent so much time together.

Relieved, I found Lisa outside standing along our attached garage talking with Dave and smoking a cigarette. I must have given her an odd look. We had both been smokers, but quit when our children were born. Lisa had recently started working full time, the first time since Madeline and Noah were born. Lisa had told me within the past month that work had been very stressful sometimes at the restaurant and she had a couple of cigarettes, especially during the really bad days. I didn't like it, but understood. I had no idea that she was smoking regularly again. I just chuckled, even during this moment of grief, and said, "Smoke 'em if you got 'em."

We walked together back inside and sat on the couch. I told her that we needed to go to the hospital and see Ashley. "I can't. I can't do it. I wish it were me. I wish it were me." Lisa sobbed. It's not normal for children to die before their parents. It's outside the natural order of things. Mom and dad are supposed to die first. Any parent wants for their children to live long, happy, prosperous and better lives than they did. They want their child to get married and give them grandchildren, to experience life. It's not fair to have life cut so short. Any parent would exchange their life for their child's. "I wish it were me." I understood that. Tears continued to run down my face. We had to go.

Deputy Johnson offered to take us to St. Vincent hospital. We were in no condition to drive. We climbed into the back seat of his unmarked squad car. The drive to the hospital seemed to take forever, but we arrived in a matter of minutes. The hospital was less than five miles from our front door. I requested that we park in the sally port, where I always parked when I arrested drunk drivers and walked them inside for a blood test. This walk was much different.

We walked through the double doors from the sally port to the emergency room. The automatic doors opened and we were met by the medical examiner. "I'm very sorry…" That's all I remember him saying.

We knew Ashley was dead. We had already been told that. Lisa sat in the hallway along the wall, just outside the OWI room. I stood alongside her. "Where is she?" I asked. He motioned to the room directly in front of us. The white curtains were drawn across the sliding glass doors that divided her room from the wide hallway. Bright lights shone from underneath the curtain, just above the floor. We couldn't see inside. There was silence that seemed to last forever. "Are you ready?" I asked. Lisa stared at the ceiling, took a deep breath, and stood up. Hand in hand, we walked toward Ashley's room. I slid the door open, drew the curtains back with my right hand and we walked past them, inside.

It seemed surreal. This can't be happening, "She shouldn't be dead," I thought to myself. Not because she was dead, but because she looked so good, from what we could see.
It was peaceful, oddly. Only three small horizontal marks, like a single rail road track, were on her left cheek. An off-white blanket covered Ashley from the chest down. Her uncovered arms lay still along her sides.

Lisa gripped Ashley's left arm. I cupped her forehead with my right hand and ran my fingers through her hair. I kissed Ashley's forehead and told her I loved her. The last words I said to her in life were now repeated in death. She felt so cold. "This isn't her..." Lisa said, tearfully, "...it's just her body."

A few months later, at Lisa's request, we would receive a copy of Ashley's autopsy report. Her neck was broken and spinal cord crushed. Extensive hemorrhage was present on the soft tissues of her chest walls. Her diaphragm was torn and all of her ribs along her left side were fractured. Her aorta was ripped from her heart and left lung was lacerated. Ashley was an organ donor and nothing could be donated. We were told she didn't have a chance and didn't suffer. Does that make the emotional pain and recovery any easier? I don't know, some say it does. This report was just another part of the story.

Our Pastor arrived and stood behind Lisa. I had no idea who had called him. I didn't even notice his presence until he started reciting some Bible verses in between what were meant to be reassuring words. He was doing what pastors are supposed to do. We would both later talk about this moment and, although very well intentioned, all we remember hearing was a voice similar to "Charlie Brown's" teacher-- muffled and distorted. Our grieving minds kept us from hearing him.

The medical examiner stood behind us, in the corner, near the open curtain. "What do you need from us?" I asked sternly and walked toward the steel cart that held his brown leather folder. Ashley's driver's license photograph seemed to peer at me from an appropriately-sized sleeve. It seemed to say, "I'm okay." Her image was reassuring. He handed me the documents and I signed a form verifying our relationship to Ashley.

Little did I know that Anrietta, the drunk driver, was in a trauma room *less than one hundred feet from us.* It's probably better that I didn't know this. The one responsible for killing Ashley and Talhia was being treated. Like so many drunk drivers, she lived. It's said that the reason drunk drivers often live through severe crashes is because they are oblivious and relaxed at impact. Instead of bracing for the crash, their bodies just absorb it. They become the human versions of the crash test dummies. Anrietta, although alive in the hospital, was also under arrest.

We walked out of Ashley's room and were escorted to the family room adjacent to the ER. In the hallway we met a stone-faced woman. Her straight, shoulder-length brown hair hung and covered her ears. Tears ran down her thin face. We knew this had to be Talhia's mother. We were right; it was Ann Heroux, Talhia's mom. Talhia and Ashley worked together at Texas Roadhouse and spent many days hanging out. Talhia had just spent the night at our house two days before. We last saw Talhia at our kitchen table indulging in pasta that Lisa had made. (She even had two helpings, a compliment to the chef.) We exchanged names and phone numbers. Grieving parents would be in touch again over the next several days.

Captain Thomas had also come to the hospital and drove us back home. We both sat in the back seat, scrunched in between a plastic tub holding necessary police equipment and the passenger side back door. A shotgun rack was at our feet. We didn't care. It was a silent ride.

Chad and Dave met us as we walked inside. "Is there anything else we can do?" they asked. For that night, there was nothing more to be done. They left a few minutes later. We just needed to be left alone and I had more phone calls to make. Noah was still sleeping and he didn't know his big sister was dead.

There was no way I could sleep and time seemed to stand still. We stayed up the rest of the night. I would not sleep for nearly

24 hours after Ashley's death. Sleep didn't seem important or even necessary.

As the morning birds chirped and sunlight filled the house, it was time to tell Noah. We woke him at about 8:00 a.m. He was Ashley's "Little Boo." Although Madeline was Ashley's sister, Noah had a special place in Ashley's heart.

Typically groggy, Noah was slow to wake. We took our time and allowed him to gather himself. A few minutes later, I walked him to our living room for the sad news; the third death notification.

Lisa couldn't face this moment and waited down the hall, by Ashley's bedroom. Madeline sat by my side. I told Noah that Ashley was dead and tried to explain why in simple terms that he would understand. I cried. Madeline cried. Noah cried. Tears ran down his face. Through his sobs and convulsive gasps he cried out, "Why, why?" It was heart breaking to hear. I heard Lisa crying in the background. I was unable to answer his question. The only thing that made sense to him at this moment was that Ashley was dead. It wasn't right! No child should be put through this emotional pain.

The emotional and psychological trauma of sudden death transforms and changes a child for life. However, we sometimes don't realize the extent of the impact that sudden death can have on the psyche of a child. It sometimes gets revealed in what they say at the moment:

"Now I guess I have to be the big sister."

I couldn't believe what I had just heard. Madeline expressed her intent to step up and fill the void created less than 12 hours ago. It broke my heart to hear these words. Madeline was indeed now the big sister.

I took a three-hour nap on the afternoon of June 4th. Little did I realize that funerals were planned in 72 hours. The planning for our "new normal," a phrase I learned to hate, began immediately.

I don't remember much about the first 30 days after Ashley's death. I was so focused on doing one thing, and that was keeping the four of us together. I was automatically given three days off for funeral leave, but there was no way I would be in any condition to go back in 72 hours. Besides the sadness and pain, Ashley's death brought back many negative childhood memories. It had taken me many years into adulthood to understand that responsible use of alcohol was possible and in many cases, normal. Until then, I perceived alcohol as purely evil because everything surrounding it in my life was negative. After all, it was alcohol that ripped the fabric of my childhood. It was, in part, why I became a cop. I had believed that I was doing the right thing, detecting and arresting drunk drivers, and preventing fatalities. I had also responded to my share of domestic violence incidents where alcohol, in nearly all cases, was a factor. The average BAC of the hundreds of drunk drivers that I had arrested in my career was .18, more than two-times the legal limit. Contrary to what many believe, the social drinker who has a "couple" of drinks with dinner or friends, is not the one getting arrested for OWI. Rather, the truly impaired and dangerous ones were. That is what I believed. But on the night of Ashley's death, there was nothing that I could have done to save her life. I felt so powerless. This was something that I couldn't control, which is difficult for a cop to accept.

Lisa and Ashley had worked together in the same downtown building. Lisa, a chef at the second floor "Quincy's" restaurant, would see Ashley most days at the "Daily Buzz" coffee shop, right below the restaurant. Lisa would always stroll into work early and take time to chat with Ashley. It was perfect for these two "best friends" and allowed them to catch up on life. Not seeing Ashley each day as she walked into work was too much for Lisa to bear. Ashley's death not only robbed Lisa of their relationship, but it eventually ended her career.

Although parenting experts say that the role of a parent is not to be a child's best friend but rather a mentor, provider, and sometimes disciplinarian, the right parenting can lead to a "best" friendship as they become adults. That is the kind of mom that Lisa was to Ashley. Not only was Ashley the first born, but until I came into their lives, it was just the two of them. Lisa and Ashley survived together and that bond only grew throughout the years. They had a unique relationship. Lisa quiet. Ashley very loud. They complemented each other well. But they were both downright goofy together.

It was typical for Lisa and Ashley to get ready to go shopping and with no planning whatsoever, wear matching outfits. They would sit together in the living room and text each other, having a little fun at my expense, even while I was in the room and just giggle. It was the laughter that always gave away what they were up to.

Lisa would often say to Ashley, "I don't know what I would do without you." She was now about to find out.

Although off duty at the time, Officer Tom Kraus was the first police officer on scene. Officer Kraus stood along the open driver's side door (below) of Anriette's Porsch and reported the crash to the 911 operator. Because of the devastation, Talhia had been pushed on top of Ashley, preventing Officer Kraus from seeing her.

Deputy Tim Johnson had the unfortunate duty of making Ashley's death notification.

Deputy Scott Vandevoort accompanied Deputy Johnson during Ashley's death notification

Captain Todd Thomas, the Green Bay Police Department Night Shift Commander at the time of Ashley's death. Captain Thomas spared no resources ensuring that we were supported that night.

Officer Dave Steffens (left) and Officer Chad Ramos (right) responded directly to our residence shortly after we were told Ashley had been killed. Both offered tremendous emotional support.

Deputy Kevin Pawlak, the traffic accident reconstructionist who worked tirelessly to ensure that the crime scene was properly reconstructed.

Deputy Art Adams assisted in the accident reconstruction and investigation.

Ashwaubenon Public Safety Lieutenant Jody Crocker, lead investigator. A photo of Ashley and Talhia sits near his desk as a daily reminder of why he's a cop.

Brown County District Attorney David Lasee, lead prosecutor who fought for justice in memory of Ashley and Talhia.

This billboard has been donated by Jag Outdoor advertising and placed along Interstate 41 between Appleton and Green Bay as a sobering reminder of the ultimate impact of drunk driving. We are forever grateful for the generosity and kindness extended by Jag Outdoor.

Brown County Deputy John Flannery (retired); Directed Patrol Officer assigned to our community at the time of Ashley's death. Deputy Flannery was our first advocate and updated us regularly as early developments unfolded.

65

Chapter VII

THE IMPACT

There was no way I would be able to return to work after my three days of funeral leave. I had accumulated many sick days over the years and figured I could just use those until I would be able to go back to work – if at all.

I wanted to quit. Everything that I had believed was questioned, from my work to my faith. Why even try to make a difference? Why bother being a police officer if you can't even prevent a child's death? Why did God allow this to happen? Why was I being punished, again? Wasn't what I grew up with enough?

During these painful hours, fellow officers were doing what they could to help make things just a little easier for us. Our lawn was cut. Food arrived in mass quantities. Gift cards were given for fuel. They also volunteered to work my shifts for the next month. I didn't have to go back to work until July 1st.

I couldn't believe it. I had heard about and seen the brother and sisterhood of police work, but now I was experiencing it firsthand. Expecting nothing in return, officers volunteered to work for me, taking time away from their families. There was no way to repay these acts of kindness. The idea of protecting and serving goes well beyond the uniform. Not having to go back to work for a month was a weight off my mind, but it would quickly be replaced by another one.

After viewing Ashley at the hospital, we had been briefly introduced to Ashwaubenon Public Safety Detective Lieutenant Jody Crocker. A tall, thin, 20-year veteran, with sandy blond hair and a moustache, Jody became our point of contact. He was our advocate and the one to ensure that justice would ultimately be served. This was no small responsibility. One legal misstep and the defendant could be set free. He would also be the bearer of all news, good and bad. We felt that Lt. Crocker was fighting for us, a feeling critical for all victims.

We were updated throughout the weekend regarding the investigation and cause of the crash. I would frequently call Lt. Crocker and question or even recommend that certain steps be taken. I was in full "cop mode" to ensure that the investigation was done right. At the time I thought if I didn't fight for Ashley, no one would.

We were told that alcohol was a factor in the crash and charges of "homicide by intoxicated use" would be pursued. High speed, in excess of 80 miles per hour, was another factor. The investigation would take weeks to complete. The last thing we were told would have more of a long-term impact. The driver and owner of the $50,000 Porsche convertible sports car, Anrietta Geske, was driving it without insurance.

I called our auto insurance company and reported Ashley's death. The representative was as empathetic as she could be. When I told her that Anrietta didn't have insurance, she assured me that our policy would provide coverage within the policy limits, which also included a $10,000 death benefit to help cover funeral expenses. I had no idea what a funeral would cost, but presumed that this benefit would offer some relief. An appointment was scheduled with an insurance adjuster to come to our house in the next couple days.

I continued to merely exist. Each day was a struggle. Chores were truly chores. Tears came often. Anger and frustration became the norm. Our days were filled with one item on our "to do" list, to merely exist.

On Wednesday, June 4, 2008, Lisa and I sat down at our house with Ken and Mary Gehm. They were about to "pay it forward" and help us through our tragedy, just as others had done for them.

Fourteen months earlier, on April 15, 2007, Ken and Mary had lost their son, Jared, to sudden death – a suicide. Ken, now a retired Green Bay Police Officer, and Mary had used Jared's death in a positive way, to bring awareness of suicide by creating the annual Green Bay Family Fun Run. This annual event raises scholarship funds for Green Bay area students who have participated in cross-country, as Jared did, and who are pursuing a college education. (Additional information regarding the Green Bay Family Fun Run is available at http://www.familyfunrun.org/)

I will never forget how I felt the day Jared died. The police department was in turmoil. During these times most people, unless they have experienced sudden death, have no idea how to react. What can you say to make it better? What can you do to help? When you see surviving family members after the funeral, what do you say to them in passing? Because people are not naturally comfortable talking about death, especially the sudden death of a child, it's easier to just avoid the subject. Often, people avoid the survivors, who in turn feel treated as though they have a contagious disease. The survivors become unintentionally quarantined. The surviving family begins to feel isolated. I never understood this until we lost Ashley.

Although I knew Ken well, until this day at the house, I had never met Mary. Ken was always positive at work and we saw eye to eye in more ways than one-- he was my height. He had been a motivated traffic officer for many years and was well liked. He was always fair and was known to take that little extra time with people. It was not uncommon for people to thank Ken, even when he gave them a ticket! Ken preferred patrol with the police Harley-Davidson motorcycle, and I always wondered how he controlled that large bike with such a small frame. Ken weighed only about 160 pounds. His short brown hair was often covered by the mandatory motorcycle helmet. Ken's positivity at work changed after Jared died. Just the mere thought of talking about Jared brought tears to his eyes and I saw them at work, more than once. Ken and I developed a bond that was cemented in loss.

"Welcome to the club that you were not invited to," said Ken. While we sat around our kitchen table, I felt comfortable talking to Ken and Mary about Jared for the first time. They shared with us how they got through their loss and stayed together. That was my focus as well, to keep us together through this. Ken and Mary stressed the importance of counseling, talking openly and frequently about Ashley, and most importantly, the power of faith. They also offered to help with funeral arrangements. A meeting with Ken at the funeral home was set.

Shortly after the Gehm's left, the insurance adjuster arrived. Unlike the representative on the phone, this adjuster was obviously uncomfortable talking to us about Ashley. I don't recall his name. He was about 30 years old, with disheveled brown hair and wire-rimmed glasses that continually slid down his face. His stammer became increasingly frustrating. We just wanted him to get through the paperwork and leave. He did his best to explain how our policy would provide some coverage but finished with, "I'm sorry to tell you this, but the $10,000 death benefit is *not* available."

I was furious! Lisa sat next to me, speechless. He tried to offer an explanation, but I wasn't in any frame of mind to hear it. It was the last thing he told us before leaving.

I immediately called my insurance agent and vented. "How can they tell us that the $10,000 death benefit is available to help cover funeral expenses and then take it away?" I demanded a response. We were already victimized again, and this time by our own insurance company! My insurance agent assured me that he would look into it and get back to me.

I received a call back within an hour from an insurance company manager. He apologized on behalf of the company and assured us the $10,000 death benefit *would* be provided. This was yet another thing we had to fight for and that wasn't right. I quickly discovered that your insurance company is always your advocate until you make a claim and they may actually have to pay you.

Chapter VIII

THE FUNERAL HOME

It's not "natural" for parents to plan a funeral for their children. Children are supposed to bury their parents. But that was not the case.

During the late morning hours of Thursday, June 5, 2008, Ken drove us to the "Proko-Wall Funeral Home" on the city's east side. I had selected them on the night of Ashley's death because of the empathetic care that I had seen them provide to other victim families at death scenes.

Unfortunately, Ken had some experience with this and helped us through the entire process, from selecting a casket to the urn that Ashley's ashes would be placed in. Ashley had discussions early in life, especially with Lisa, regarding death. It was almost like she knew she was going to die young. It's not often that a teenager expresses her wish to be cremated. Ashley had also written a poem that spoke of her life, "In the Sky."

In the Sky   April 20, 2004

The days I look up to the sky
I stand up straight, look up high, and wonder why
Why so many people here on earth
Act like nothing is from God; their own turf.
The days I constantly wonder
What lies ahead
The times I ponder
About the dead
The dead that lived a life with Him
They ran the race
Their heads now are crowned.
The highest victory it must be
To run the race, win, and be set free

To be with Him is one thought --
One thought that will never leave my mind
For in time, I will be up there
In the sky.

Ashley Knetzger

All three of us sat at a wooden table with the funeral director.
We had no idea what to expect. The necessary paperwork was
explained and we were asked, "Do you want a viewing..."
Lisa interrupted him and made it very clear that there would
be a viewing and then Ashley would be cremated, per her
wishes. This was duly noted. The urn selection was next.
Lisa excused herself and went to the bathroom.

While Lisa was away, a selection of urns was brought out,
about five of them. I don't recall what they all looked like, but
one stood out. An awful salmon pink urn with light pink
swirls, shades of lighter and darker pink hues. This urn was a
beacon among the others. None of the others stood out like
this one. Are they really supposed to stand out?

I thought to myself, "The pink one is out," and as I was about
to tell them to get rid of it Lisa returned and exclaimed, "Oh
my God! That's it, that's the one!"

The look on my face said, "Seriously?"

"Yes! Ashley would love it," Lisa replied.

Even in death, Ashley's sense of humor was present. Loud,
obnoxious, and the center of it all, but this time in the form of
a salmon-colored urn.

The funeral director then presented us with a final option; a
unique way to remember Ashley. Ken spoke up, "Mike &
Lisa, I have one to remember Jared, his thumb print pressed
into a silver medallion that can be worn on a necklace."

We ordered four of them, one for each of us. It is one way that we can still hold a part of Ashley's hand or carry her with us all the time.

As a parent, you never realize the impact that you can have on a child, sadly, until they are gone. The measure of a parent is not what your child says to you, but rather what they say about you to others when you're not around. I was very aware of my absence due to police work and other part-time jobs; always trying to do what was right for Ashley and her future. After her death, I wondered, *what kind of person would she have become? What type of nurse would she become? How did I do as a dad?* These questions were answered by others who shared with us stories about Ashley. The lead hostess at Texas Roadhouse that hired and worked with Ashley wrote,

During her orientation, Ashley asked me what I did "outside of work" and I told her that I attended school. "Where?" She asked. "I go to ITT Tech," I replied. I remember this so clearly...I was filling out her I-9. I can still see it in my mind. Ashley was squirming in her seat, she was so excited, and I couldn't figure out why. "My dad teaches there!" She almost yelled it. "What do you go to school for?" She asked. "Criminal justice," I replied. "Do you know Mike Knetzger? He's my dad." I said that I did not. She spent the next 20 minutes talking about her dad, the "brilliant" Mike, who was a police officer, a teacher, a writer, a black belt, a genius. Then it was time to talk about her understanding beautiful mom Lisa who was her "best friend, but more, and a great person."

The letter continued…

I remember one night she came in and began telling me this story about her dad, and within minutes the entire host stand was gathered around. She was telling us that her dad had

73

responded to a call the day before about a man with a knife, and to hear her tell this story, her dad was John McClane or Jack Bauer, single handedly wrestling the perp down. I remember she ended that story with, "I'm so proud of my dad."

The letter brought tears to my eyes. I felt like the hand of God patted me on the back and said, "Job well done." Oh, by the way, the guy with the knife…I had some help taking him into custody. My yellow electronic control device was deployed when he reached for a boot knife. He fell straight back, onto the asphalt parking lot. Once the handcuffs were on he apologized and was promptly taken to jail.

A supervisor at the nursing home where Ashley earned her hours for her Certified Nursing Assistant (CNA) license gave us a glimpse into the type of nurse that she would have become.

There was this elderly resident who would never eat his dinner. Somehow Ashley got him to eat. She used the power of humor. He enjoyed Ashley's company and would always laugh at her silly jokes.

Humor can have healing qualities. It also increases positive emotions. After all, it's hard to dislike somebody who makes you laugh. Ashley understood that and used it well. She also embraced the universal life value and valued all people simply because they were human. Ashley had already begun to make a difference in the lives of others. She would have been a wonderful nurse.

Friday, June 6, 2008 – Ashley's Final Goodbye

Ashley's funeral was set for a four-hour viewing followed by a church service the next day at Immanuel Lutheran Church in

Shirley, WI. Immanuel was a small country church with a two room school house that we had stumbled upon. A year earlier, we had been looking for a new school for Madeline and Noah and "Google" directed us to Immanuel. The day we toured it and met with the principle and teacher, who was the same person, I once again incorrectly judged Lisa's perspective. The church and school was 17 minutes from our door step to theirs. It was literally in the country, surrounded by farms. There was no way, I thought, that Lisa would like it. As we walked out of the church and school, I sat in our car and began to speak, "Well, I suppose you..." Lisa interrupted me, "I love it!" It was the small atmosphere, personal attention, and genuine approach that she thought was perfect for Madeline and Noah. Lisa's perception was spot-on and that is where Madeline and Noah continued and finished grade school. Although "Google" provided us with direction, God ultimately led us there.

I had no idea how many people to expect at Ashley's visitation. The Green Bay Police Department honor guard stood watch at entrances and provided direction. We were the first to view Ashley that day and would eventually be the last, several hours later.

Friends, extended family, police officers in uniform and out, and even some of her favorite customers from Texas Road House came through the line that day to show respect and thank us for allowing Ashley into their lives. Over a thousand people viewed Ashley that day. The line never seemed to end.

Although Ashley was not given "full police honors," it sure felt that way. I was honored that so many fellow warriors showed respect for Ashley. The current police academy class, whom I was supposed to teach the morning after Ashley's death, came through the line. All stood at attention while, one-by-one, they stepped forward to view her. I will never forget that sight.

I also discovered for the first time in my life that you can actually run out of tears. I cried so much that eventually, although still crying, no tears came.

Visitation went beyond the scheduled end time. Once over, we were allowed to spend time alone with Ashley. It was so quiet as we stood along her right side. As I faced Ashley, behind me, to my left and right were flowers of every color interspersed with photo boards and some of Ashley's favorite mementos. One stood out; her tennis racquet that had been inserted into and made part of a bouquet.

For some reason, at this moment I thought to myself, "Ashley, you are so brave. Through no choice of your own, you have walked through the valley of death."

Even though I walk through the darkest valley, I will fear no evil, for you are with me; your rod and your staff, they comfort me. Psalm 23:4

What Ashley endured was so much more than the risks that I take and expose myself to each day as a police officer. The meaning and value of life – ALL LIFE – meant so much more at this moment. I often said to Ashley, Madeline, and Noah, "Always appreciate what you have and don't take life for granted. It can all be gone in an instant." I just never thought that would happen to one of us. I don't use that quote anymore. I don't need to remind Madeline and Noah of that. They get it.

The next morning, we arrived at Immanuel Lutheran Church about a half-hour early. The funeral was set to start at 10:30 a.m. We were allowed to see Ashley, alone, for the last time. There wasn't much left to say or think. Nothing would bring Ashley back. No prayers at that moment would take away the pain. A large cross overlooked the church and Jesus, hung from it, peered down on Ashley. More flowers, at her head

76

and feet. "Why do people bring or send so many flowers," I thought, "What are we going to do with all of these?" It's strange what goes through your mind during grief.

Even though I was confident that I had done all I could for Ashley in life, I often wondered if it had been enough. Could I have done more? All of those little things that sometimes annoyed us, like her overwhelming – at times - loud and obnoxious personality were already missed. The extra hours that I had to work to send her to private schools were all worth it. I had no regrets. I was confident that she was in heaven with her savior, Jesus Christ. In the face of this confidence, I still asked, "Why God, why did you let this happen? What am I supposed to do with this?" The answer would come later.

The church quickly reached the 150 person capacity. It became standing room only at the back, into hallways, and the only two classrooms. Again, the show of support was overwhelming.

I don't remember much about the church service itself. It was surreal. It took a mere 40 minutes to end Ashley's funeral. This marked the end for many, but merely our new beginning.

An anonymous donor paid for Ashley's grave space. Yet another act of kindness that we can never repay. We had been prepared to pay for Ashley's space and, instead, used the funds to buy our own, right next to her. Her death was a somber reminder that our next breath is never guaranteed. Purchasing our grave space made that even more apparent.

For the next couple of weeks, I continued to make phone calls to Lt. Crocker, sometimes multiple calls per day. I needed updates on the case. Were Anrietta's blood results back yet? What was her BAC? Was she in jail yet or still in the hospital? Was the reconstruction done yet?

77

I was so focused on ensuring justice for Ashley, that I wasn't taking the time to grieve and be a dad to Madeline and Noah or a husband to Lisa. I didn't even realize this until I received a brutally honest phone call.

"Hello," I answered. It was from a restricted number and I don't recall exactly who he was, but I clearly remember what he said.

"Mike, you need to stop acting like a cop. Let the system work. You need to grieve and be there for Lisa, Madeline, and Noah."

He was right! I needed to hear that. The four of us, we were most important at this time, and needed to focus on each other to get through this. I knew I couldn't do it alone. I needed help.

Like many businesses and entities these days, the City of Green Bay offered an "Employee Assistant Program" (EAP), which included free counseling. I was aware that other cops had used the EAP, but the feedback was rarely positive. I also knew, however, that cops can be difficult to counsel. We are not ones to just trust others or, for that matter, "surrender" ourselves to a counselor and admit that we need help. It's contrary to what we do every day. Plus the police image says, "I can handle anything." If we do admit that we need help, we don't trust any counselor unless they have "been there" before. Because of this cultural attitude problem, some of the most successful "cop counselors" are former cops.

I had no idea what to do for Madeline or Noah. I had no idea what to do for Lisa to make this better. I had no idea what to do to keep all of us together. This was something that I couldn't handle. I needed help.

Within the first week of Ashley's death, the four of us sat down with our EAP counselor. I have trouble remembering much about her appearance or sound of her voice. I do recall that her name was Cheryl and she had lived in Virginia before relocating to Green Bay. Cheryl was an experienced counselor, a bit older than us. After the first session, me and Lisa were assigned to Cheryl and Madeline and Noah were seen by a specialist that counseled children.

Cheryl shared her east coast perspective of alcohol use. "In Virginia," Cheryl explained, "when we went out for a couple of drinks, that meant two. We never drove drunk; the drunk driver was shunned. In Wisconsin, I have discovered that "a couple" has a different meaning. It's the only place where you can order a couple *buckets* of beer. Alcohol is a pervasive problem. Driving drunk is like a rite of passage.

Cheryl confirmed what I already knew. How can this Wisconsin cultural perspective be changed? Can we arrest our way out of the problem? We have tried that with the so-called, *War on Drugs*, and there must be a better way. Changing this cultural perspective and savings lives became a goal, but it wouldn't be easy.

Cheryl also explained that it would take us up to three years to find our "new normal" and how we are going to live on without Ashley. "Three years!" I couldn't believe it! It had just been a matter of weeks and every day was filled with pain and sadness. I couldn't fathom three years down the road. At this point, each day was a struggle.

As our counseling progressed, twice a week, Cheryl offered perspectives that we couldn't see due to the dark clouds of emotion that often engulfed us. My recollections of how she specifically helped us are fragmented. The one consistent recollection? Tears, crying, anger, frustration, and more tears. The last session, however, near the end of June and a few days before I was scheduled to go to back to work was most memorable.

Cheryl's counseling office contained her desk and two chairs along a wall with no barrier in between her and the clients. Our chairs were cushioned and somewhat comfortable. A small table was in between me and Lisa, upon which a Kleenex box sat.

On this day, Lisa sat to my right. I had thoughts of not returning to work and retiring on a psychological disability. The mere thought that I would have to return to work in a few days caused great anxiety. *How would I handle the next drunk driver? Would I be able to do it?* I had never felt or experienced anxiety like this before. My heart rate would increase and I could feel internal shaking. There was no way I could function, I thought, on the streets in this condition.

I said to Cheryl, "I don't think I can go back to work." I continued and described the terrible anxiety at the mere thought of it.

Cheryl replied, "Mike, that is totally understandable. You could probably retire on a psychological disability. I would have to refer you to a psychiatrist, medications would be prescribed, and you could get 60 to 80 percent of your salary as disability. But before we do that, let me ask you a question."

There was a few seconds of silence. Cheryl asked, "What would Ashley want you to do?"

Lisa squeezed my right hand. My chin quivered. Tears ran down my face. I replied, "She would want me to go out there and kick some ass!"

Cheryl said, "Then why don't you do that? Go about and make a difference in Ashley's name."

I was so angry. The answer was so easy. Do what I can to make a difference. That is what God wanted me to do with this. I decided to go back to work. To serve and protect. To make a difference, in Ashley's name and memory.

Chapter IX

THE NEXT DRUNK DRIVER

I went back to work on July 2, 2008. I reported for roll call at 7:00 p.m. The mood was somber. I was welcomed back. The guys were glad I came back. So was I, but I knew it wouldn't be easy. I still wondered how I would handle the next drunk driver. It didn't take long to find out.

At approximately 11:30 p.m., I was dispatched to assist Captain Thomas, who had brought us home from the hospital after viewing Ashley four weeks ago. He had stopped a drunk driver in downtown Green Bay.

While en route, my pulse quickened and I took deep breaths, in through my nose and out of my mouth, to help reduce the anxiety. I arrived a few minutes later and Captain Thomas explained why he stopped the guy. He handed me the driver's license and also told me that it would be this man's second offense.

I had the suspect exit his vehicle and escorted him to the back of his car. I patted him for any weapons and saw a "Latin King" gang tattoo on his right forearm. In the next few moments, he made me aware that he was a gang member and didn't like police. I was able to convince him to participate in the standard field sobriety tests. While I was examining his eyes with the horizontal gaze nystagmus test, my left index finger shook as I moved it from side-to-side in front of him. It was evident that he was impaired. All of the clues were there: the lack of smooth tracking as the eyes hesitated while following my finger, bouncing while in the corners. Even if he had refused to do the other tests, I was still going to arrest him. He had admitted to the typical "couple" of drinks with slurred speech. I don't recall how he performed on the one-leg stand or the walk-and-turn, but he was arrested for drunk driving. He didn't resist, but he made his disdain for police clear.

I requested that another squad meet me at the hospital, anticipating some resistance from him. I was right; he didn't consent to the blood draw. Since it was his second offense, a misdemeanor traffic offense, it was our policy to force the blood draw. All necessary and reasonable force was permitted to obtain this blood evidence, with the blood alcohol level dropping with each passing moment. He made it clear that nobody was going to take his blood. Hospital security was called and they arrived a few minutes later with restraints. The presence of security and police convinced him to cooperate, and although he objected, he didn't resist and the blood was drawn.

The suspect willingly walked to my squad car parked in the emergency room garage. He continued to blame me for his arrest. Apparently, it was all my fault that he drove drunk. As I drove to the jail, his vulgarity and insults began to wear on me. About five minutes away from the jail, my patience came to an end and I spoke up.

"Hey!" I said, "Do you have any kids?"

He replied, "Yeah, why?"

I continued, "What do you have, a boy or a girl?

"A girl," he revealed, and I asked her age. "Two," he said.

I continued, "Look at it this way, you will get out of jail tomorrow and be able to see your daughter again. Thirty days ago, I lost my 18-year-old daughter to a drunk driver, no different than you."

There was complete silence. Then he began to cry. I couldn't believe this "bad-ass" gang member was crying in the back seat of my squad car!

Neither of us spoke for the rest of the ride. I parked my squad car in the jail garage, secured my handgun, electric weapon, and baton in the trunk, and then opened the back passenger side door.

The drunk driver looked at me with tears running down his face. "Officer," he asked, "can you wipe the tears from my eyes so the guys in the jail don't see me crying?"

I carry a roll of toilet paper with me. It's the highest quality toilet paper that government can buy, like fine-grain sandpaper. I use it frequently during allergy season. I grabbed a sheet, wiped the tears from his eyes, and assisted him out of the squad. I escorted him into the booking area and he remained silent. I filled out the booking form and indicated OWI – Second Offense. The correctional officer completed a thorough search of the drunk driver and told me that I could remove the handcuffs.

I took off the handcuffs and then turned in my booking form. I was told that the paperwork was in order and I could leave. Just as I reached for the steel door that separates the booking or intake area from the garage, I heard a voice.

"Officer," the drunk driver said to me. I turned toward him as he slowly approached me. His shoulders were rolled forward and his head hung low. He extended his right hand toward me and said, "I'm sorry."

I shook his hand and replied, "It's okay, just don't do it again."

I walked into the garage toward my squad car and thought about how a glimpse of Ashley's story - at this very moment - made a difference in this gang member's life. Could it make a difference in the lives of others as well?

This is where *Ashley's Story* began.

Chapter X

THE JURY TRIAL

A week after Ashley and Talhia were murdered by that 2,000 pound speeding bullet driven by Anrietta Geske, the drunk driver made her initial appearance in Brown County (WI) circuit court.

Due to the nature and extent of her lower extremity injuries, Anrietta was hospitalized for the week and appeared in front of the judge in a wheelchair. She was covered from the neck down with a white sheet, so the extent of her injuries wouldn't be given consideration. Anrietta pled not guilty to the charges of homicide by intoxicated use, first degree reckless homicide, and recklessly endangering safety. Bail was set at $500,000 and she was returned to the hospital. The criminal court process had officially begun.

We had become aware of the evidence. After Anrietta had been extricated from her Porsche and was inside the ambulance, an officer asked her how much she had had to drink. She provided the typical answer: "A couple." The officer smelled an odor of intoxicants emitting from Anrietta. She blew a quick breath into a Preliminary Breath Test (PBT) unit and she was at .086 – just above the legal .08 limit. A longer breath sample would likely have yielded a higher result. Was her blood alcohol level increasing or decreasing? Nobody could know at this point. No other field sobriety tests could be administered. The more time that passed from the time of the crash to obtaining Anrietta's evidentiary blood sample, the lower it would probably be.

Two hours after the crash, the blood sample was obtained and the official evidentiary result was a .072, below the conclusive prima facia standard. Prima facia evidence stands on its own and, without question, proves a fact. Without it, we now had to rely upon experts to help determine what Anrietta's BAC was at the time of the crash. An expert witness from the crime lab was contacted and applied the principle of retrograde extrapolation. This scientific theory uses the known hourly rate of alcohol dissipation, an average of .015 per hour, with the amount of time that passed between operating a motor vehicle and the blood draw. The expert concluded that Anrietta's BAC at the time of crash was .107, well above the legal limit. The expert also testified that a second analysis of Anrietta's blood detected levels of her prescription medication that had known negative interactions with alcohol, likely increasing impairment.

Some time prior to the jury trial, Anrietta had been offered a plea agreement. In exchange for a guilty plea, prosecutors would recommend a sentence of 30 years confinement followed by ten years of extended supervision. The assistant district attorney Tom Coaty asked me if we would agree to this plea agreement. I replied, "I have no idea what the hell justice means anymore. If it spares us a jury trial, then so be it." We just wanted this to end.

Ashley's death not only caused great psychological and emotional pain, it also threw into question everything I had believed about justice. Whether the offer was accepted or rejected, it wouldn't change a thing. The damage was done. Ashley was gone and no measure of justice would bring her back.

Anrietta rejected the plea and opted for a jury trial. She didn't qualify for a public defender; most people driving a Porsche wouldn't. Our family attorney discovered that she had received $50,000 in a recent divorce settlement, but this went to pay for her attorney. There was nothing left for us to pursue.

While the wheels of justice were in motion, our family attorney paid close attention and prepared the groundwork for any civil recourse. We discovered early on that Anrietta had returned to the area from Texas. That southern state was our starting point. We needed to find out all we could about her, especially potential assets that might be pursued to help compensate for our loss. For whatever reason, I recalled a conversation that I had with a man on an airplane about five years earlier whose brother worked for the Dallas Police Department. He gave me his brother's name and phone number and told me that if I ever needed anything in Dallas to give him a call.

There is a special bond between police officers, not just the ones we work with, but often across the country, simply because we are cops. I called the Dallas police officer and shared with him the sad news of Ashley's death. I began to explain the type of information that I was looking for about Anrietta and told him where she had last lived in Texas. The officer interrupted me by saying, "Mike, you're not going to believe this-- that is where I live, in that same community."

Too often we never realize the meaning or value of a chance meeting. A chance meeting on an airplane led me to a Dallas police officer who got all the information that we needed within 72 hours! No private detective. No costs to incur. He got us the information because it was the right thing to do. Unfortunately, he also discovered that Anrietta didn't have any assets. None! The Porsche was the only asset she once had and that instrument of death was totaled.

The jury trial began in Brown County (WI) Circuit Court on Monday March 16, 2009 at 8:00 a.m. It would begin at this same time each day for the next six days. Veteran Circuit Court Judge Sue Bischel presided. She was a judge known to be stern but fair. Very decisive, when Judge Bischel spoke, people listened. Her black robe and contrasting blonde hair stood out. She often made decisions or rulings while staring over prescription silver-framed glasses while pointing at target of her message. Her loud and clear voice conveyed the message clearly. Highly intelligent, very few of her cases had ever been overturned by an appellate court – the sign of a good judge. Judge Bischel was nearing retirement and this would be one of her last, most memorable cases.

Throughout my career, I had testified at many preliminary hearings and trials. I knew what to expect, but this time I was a victim rather than one of the participants. My family members were the victims and all we could do was sit and watch. We had no control or influence over the outcome. We had to trust that justice would prevail and that wasn't easy to do.

A seasoned victim advocate, Karen Doreau, was by our side and always available. Karen had been our advocate from the moment the district attorney got the case. After each court hearing, from the initial appearance, preliminary hearing, motion hearings, to the day the trial started, Karen called to explain the results of each proceeding and the next step. Loving. Caring. Passionate. Direct. Karen exemplified these traits and cared enough to form a bond with us. Even though I was very familiar with the judicial process, Karen always provided a full explanation. I was convinced that this is how she treated all crime victims. Karen was also our buffer from the media. We didn't wish to give interviews and Karen conveyed the message. She even gave us "escape routes" out of the court house each day to avoid the microphones and cameras. Karen – our advocate – made a difference.

Due to all the pretrial publicity, the jury had been selected and brought in from Eau Claire (WI), a city at the far western side of the state. The jury of twelve, plus two alternates, took their seats in the jury box. It was a balanced combination of men and women of varying ages, from their early 20s to late 60s.

Each day, Lisa and I sat in the front row along with Talhia's mom, Ann. We also had police officers accompany us. Our front row seat was at the right side of the courtroom, behind the prosecutor's table. Anrietta sat diagonally to our left, about 20 feet away. There was always a deputy positioned halfway in between us and Anrietta. That was probably a good thing. I now really understood the internal rage and anger that victims feel toward those who have caused the ultimate harm to their family members. The jury box was directly in front of us, slightly offset to our right.

Day 1 – Monday

The first day went as planned. There were opening and closing statements. Because the state had the burden of proof, they went first and articulated to the jury why Anrietta was guilty of first degree reckless homicide, homicide by intoxicated use, homicide with a prohibited alcohol concentration, and recklessly endangering safety. Guilt beyond a reasonable doubt is a high burden of proof. For the most serious charges, it had to be shown that Anrietta had utter disregard for the lives of Ashley and Talhia when she killed them. They also had to prove that she killed them while under the influence of alcohol and/or drugs. Anrietta's defense claimed it was a mere accident.

The first day of the trial seemed to go quickly. The initial responding officers had testified and although we were aware of the facts, it was different hearing them describe the scene in their own words. The smells: gasoline, anti-freeze, and the odor of intoxicants. The sounds: Anrietta moaning in pain and Ashley and Talhia: moaning in the throes of death. The sights: cars crushed, traffic control standard down, fluids all over, even a small dog. The police witnesses did their best to describe the devastation.

"The Porsche was protruded so far (into the Buick) that it caused the back tires to come up ...It was – in my 20 years of experience ...the most damage done to a vehicle that I have ever seen."

"The wreckage ...was devastating and significantly more than normal."

"It was the worst wreck that I had ever seen"

We went home that night, exhausted, as though we'd just been through a fight or boxing match. The state fought for us, and for now, we appeared to be winning the match.

Day 2 - Tuesday

At 8:00 a.m., we took our seats at the front. The morning progressed with more testimony from police officers and included some prescription medication evidence that had been found on the passenger side floor of Anrietta's Porsche. The medication was still contained in the same pharmacy bag where they were found. The prosecution asked the police witness, "Let's see what's in the bag."

The defense attorney shouted "Objection!" He not only objected to the display of this evidence, but also requested a mistrial. His basis? This was the first time, he claimed, that he became aware of this evidence-- it had not been turned over by the state in his discovery motion or demand. Discovery requires the state to turn over all evidence that will be used at trial so the defendant can prepare an adequate defense. A violation of discovery is significant.

I knew what this all meant. If it were true and the state wanted to proceed with using the evidence, a mistrial would likely be granted and we would start all over again. My heart sank.

91

Anger brewed inside.

Thoughts raced through my head: How could this happen? We can't go through this again! When will the victims stop getting victimized? But this time it was the system causing the victimization. The same system where I had often played a role.

Judge Bischel called for a recess and met with the defense and prosecution. Sure enough, a clerical error at the Ashwaubenon Public Safety Department (APSD) was the cause of this upheaval. When the drug test results arrived at the APSD, a copy was never forwarded to the DA's office. In turn, it wasn't included in all the reports that were given to Anrietta's attorney.

The prosecutors now had a decision to make. Start over or proceed with the case, excluding the prescription drug evidence while trying to get a conviction using the alcohol as the sole basis of impairment. We wouldn't know what was going to happen next until after lunch.

We didn't eat much. We were emotionally and physically sick. Time seemed to stand still. We couldn't fathom having to start the trial process over again. We just wanted all of this over with so we could keep moving toward our so-called "new normal."

Shortly after 1:00 p.m., a decision was made. To avoid the risk of a mistrial or the case being overturned on appeal, prosecutors decided to proceed without introducing the prescription drug evidence. Anrietta's blood alcohol level and driving behavior would be used to show "utter disregard" for Ashley's and Talhia's lives. It was a calculated risk.

The case continued with more descriptive testimony from officers and citizen witnesses. By the end of the day, we had heard enough.

Days 3 & 4 – Wednesday and Thursday

The trial proceeded as planned, including our routine. Up early. Decompression breaths to help alleviate stress and anxiety. Slow walks to the courthouse to take our front row seats.

I believe the jury figured out that we were the parents of either Ashley or Talhia. The jury member closest to us, at the near end of the jury box, was a gray haired woman in her late 60s. She was short and thin, and often glanced at us. She was probably somebody's grandmother, I thought. She had a calm and confident look. She listened intently and, like all the jurors, never spoke…until later.

Elizabeth, the passenger in the car that drag raced against Anrietta, also testified. Her testimony was consistent with the written statement she had provided to police. Elizabeth was obviously nervous, like any teen would be in such a high-profile trial. She accurately and compassionately told the jury what she saw and described the speed of Anrietta's Porsche, at least 80 MPH, faster than any car she had ever seen [on a city street]. Elizabeth also painted a picture of a driver, Anrietta, who didn't have a care in the world as she leaned back in her seat and the rushing wind blew through her hair just before killing Ashley and Talhia.

As Elizabeth exited the courtroom she collapsed, overcome with emotion and stress.

Although these days didn't include any other legal drama, they dragged on. Jury trials are very different from what you might see on television. Although witnesses tell the story, they are often interrupted with legal objections, defense attorney perspectives and lines of questioning that open up wounds.

The defense attempted to paint the picture or excuse the behavior as merely an "accident." The only objective evidence, according to the defense, was the low BAC. Anrietta's defense completely ignored the driving behavior.

Two accident reconstruction experts, one from the Brown County Sheriff's Department and another from the Wisconsin State Patrol, did their own analysis and investigation. Their results were consistent and the estimated speed of Anrietta's Porsche at the time of the crash was either 79-96 MPH or 80-86 MPH, with the most probable speed being 87 MPH.

Anrietta would in turn have her opportunity to present her perspective and attempt to persuade the jury that this was just an accident.

Day 5 - Friday

Anrietta's defense also called an expert to refute the findings that she had been driving at least 79 MPH at the time of the crash. Sadly, money can buy any opinion. Her expert proposed that the Porsche was traveling "only" between 50-55 MPH and the lower front end of it lifted up the Buick, like a wheel barrow, rolled with it for 126 feet, and then set it down. This not only defied logic, but the laws of gravity as well. The expert even brought red and blue foam cars that were used as props to show the jury his opinion of how the crash happened. It was hard to sit through. It was evident that Anrietta was trying to purchase her freedom.

Then one of the most difficult moments of the trial came. Anrietta decided to take the stand in her own defense. It was troubling and disgusting to sit through and listen to her testimony, which Judge Bischel later described as, "...not remotely believable."

Just as on the night that Ashley was killed and the deputies knocked on my door, anger consumed me as I listened to Anrietta's testimony. At no time did she take accountability for her actions. Instead, she used an excuse similar to a child who tells a teacher that the dog ate their homework. Anrietta blamed her dog for the crash!

Anrietta testified that she reached down (to the passenger side) toward her Chihuahua dog, which caused her foot to "tap" the gas pedal. She continued, "Since it's a fast car, I didn't expect my foot to go down when I reached [for the dog]."

I couldn't believe it! "The dog ate my homework defense!" That's the best that she could come up with!

At no time, until sentencing, did Anietta show any remorse or accountability for her actions. When she did, it was suspect and an effort to save herself from a harsh sentence. She never referred to Ashley and Talhia by name and, instead, identified them as, "those girls." Her testimony opened up more wounds, forcing us to experience the emotional pain and anger that we had experienced many times since Ashley's death.

Day 6 - Saturday

The jury had the case and was deliberating Anrietta's fate. They started at 8:00 a.m. We waited at the police department break room, two blocks from the courthouse. Would she be found guilty? If not, what could we do? Will justice be served? We pondered and expressed all of these questions. No matter the outcome, Ashley wasn't coming home again. We couldn't sit for long, and at least once an hour we went for a walk around the block. The walks helped ease some anxiety, but only temporarily. Five hours later, at about 1:00 p.m., we were told that the jury had reached a verdict.

We slowly walked along South Adams Street. We passed a law office and a church. I prayed silently for justice. My heart raced, pounding in my chest. Lisa was to my left. We held hands and she squeezed mine as we walked up the courthouse steps. At that moment, two geese, side by side, flew directly overhead, just fifty feet above us.

The goose is often synonymous with silliness, not unlike Ashley's personality and sense of humor. But also like Ashley, geese are always faithful and stand by their friends' sides, especially when they have fallen. It's well documented that during migration to a warmer climate one goose will break off and stay behind with an injured goose until it is well enough to continue or they take their final breath. They also project bravery, confidence, protection, and like Christians, fellowship.

We both squeezed each other's hands and believed this divine moment was a sign that it was all going to be okay.

We took our front row seats. The jury entered and also took their seats. The jury foreman handed their decision to the court clerk. Judge Bischel received the verdict from the clerk and read it aloud.

"We the jury, find the defendant, Anrietta Geske, guilty…" I bowed my head and tears ran down my face. This was finally over!

Anrietta was found guilty of homicide by intoxicated use (two counts), first degree reckless homicide (two counts), and recklessly endangering safety (one count). She was found not guilty of operating with a prohibited alcohol content. The jury, I presume, gave the most weight to the .072 blood result analysis, taken about two hours after the crash, and didn't believe that she necessarily had a prohibited alcohol content at the time of the crash. Most importantly, Anrietta was found guilty of the most serious charges, which carried a maximum of 30 years in prison for each count.

The finding of guilty of first degree reckless homicide was significant. The jury believed that Anrietta had displayed "utter disregard" for human life when she murdered Ashley and Talhia. It was clear that at the time of the crash, Anrietta had a depraved mind that lacked moral sense and appreciation for life, and demonstrated an unreasonable lack of judgment. Anrietta had no regard for human life at that moment on June 3, 2008.

Anrietta exercised her right to "poll" the jury. This legal procedure requires each juror to announce "guilty" or "not guilty" to each charge. Defendants hope that one jury member will say "not guilty" to one of the charges that they had just been convicted of to demonstrate that the jury wasn't unanimous.

We listened to each juror say, "guilty" 59 times as each was individually asked on each count in the case how they found the defendant. The sixtieth "guilty" was the most satisfying.

The grandmotherly woman, who had sat closest to us, after being asked, "On count 5, recklessly endangering safety, how do you find the defendant?" She looked directly at us, nodded in agreement and confidently announced, "GUILTY!"

The jurors had done their civic duty, listened to and weighed all of the evidence, and came to the only reasonable conclusion: that Anrietta was criminally responsible for murdering Ashley and Talhia.

Monday, May 11, 2009 - Sentencing

It was finally time for us to speak. Some victims choose not to make an impact statement. It's emotionally wrenching, but I had to do it. I had to speak for Ashley.

97

I took the witness stand, the same one where Anrietta had sat when she blamed her dog for the crash. Lisa, Madeline, and Noah stood behind me. I had spent hours writing the statement trying to find the words to describe the impact of Ashley's death.

I looked and spoke directly at Anrietta...

"You took our first born child..."

"You prevented many others from experiencing Ashley's warmth, her sense of humor, her overwhelming presence, and her willingness to make a difference."

"You have...

Anrietta then interrupted me and shouted, "I didn't murder those two girls!"

SLAM! SLAM! Judge Bischel swung her gavel and pointed directly at Anrietta. She made it very clear to Anrietta that it wasn't her turn to talk. Judge Bischel also made it known that she would soon have her turn to tell Anrietta how she feels and she should be concerned about THAT!

Through tears, I finished the victim impact statement. It was then Judge Bischel's turn to speak.

The impartial judge could finally express her opinion of Anrietta. Judge Bischel was blunt and made it very clear how she felt about her. This is my best recollection of Judge Bischel's most poignant opinion of Anrietta.

You perjured yourself on the stand. You offered a ridiculous, selfish, laughable, not remotely believable, manufactured story about taking care of your dog, which caused the death of two innocent girls.

98

Four years later, three Wisconsin appeals court judges would affirm Judge Bischel's decision and said, "It wasn't unreasonable to conclude that (Anrietta) Geske falsely testified that she inadvertently accelerated through a red light because she was reaching for her little dog."

The sentence was handed down.

60 YEARS PRISON

20 YEARS EXTENDED SUPERVISION

So, this was justice. This justice helped us realize that somebody was fighting for us. The police officers. Prosecutors. Victim Advocates. In the end, the judge. The system worked as intended. Justice wouldn't bring Ashley back, but it would prevent Anrietta from killing again. Justice also sent a message that this behavior wouldn't be tolerated by society at large.

EPILOGUE

On the night of June 4, 2008, Lisa and I sat at our kitchen table. The past 24 hours were a blur. We were surrounded by a few friends and one in particular was Jeremy Muraski (left). A great friend and two years younger, Jeremy often referred to me as his big brother, although I often looked up to him. Not because I'm a bit shorter, but because of his high intellect and technological skills. We had worked the Power Shift together for many years and some of our best ideas came together while we were sitting side-by-side in squad cars. He was always clean shaven and didn't have my "gift" of growing a five-o-clock shadow by noon each day.

We were reminiscing about times with and memories of Ashley. As expected, everybody's tone was somber and sadness hung in the air. We were then suddenly startled by a mouse! It dashed out from underneath our stove, ran to Stinky's food dish, stole a nugget, and ran back under the stove. I flinched and pointed. Everybody watched and then burst out in laughter. It was the first time that we had laughed in the past day. I felt guilty for laughing. It didn't seem right. But for that moment I also felt just a little bit better. The positive emotion that laughter brought didn't last long, but it was a quick reminder of its power.

A year later, Jeremy sent us an email that reflected on this moment. He reminded us of Ashley's sense of humor and the laughter, like the mouse, that she brought to our lives and others. He was right! Ashley wants us to laugh and enjoy life. Although I have always embraced the power of humor, the true power of it was revealed then and continues today. Grasp the power of humor. Use it daily. It's the cheapest and safest way to increase positive emotions, and also helps get us through the most difficult times.

Ashley taught me so much about life and death. Ashley allowed me to be a dad and gave me the privilege and opportunity to do all I could to make a difference in her life. I felt that giving her a better life than mine was what I should do as a dad. Ashley's death also reminded me of the stark reality that our next breath is not guaranteed and we must appreciate each day given to us. Although the sun may rise each morning, our body may not. Ashley's death gave me renewed commitment to life, my family, my career, and toward making a difference in the lives of others.

Dads don't hear it enough, but we do make a difference. Sometimes we discover it years later when our kids become adults. Sometimes we discover it after a death, when others report what our kids say about us when we aren't around. I was blessed to be Ashley's dad.

At the time of this writing, Ashley's Story has been shared with over 20,000 high school students, members of the armed forces, the Green Bay Packers Organization, and law enforcement officers throughout Wisconsin, New Hampshire, Minnesota, and Kansas.

Since Ashley's death, Green Bay Police Officers have arrested more than 6,000 drunk drivers within the city limits, an average of 850 arrests per year, and two-times more than years prior to her death. The average BAC of these drunk drivers - .18. The hard work and dedication of these officers has saved lives, including the reduction to only one drunk driving related fatality in 2013 and two in 2014. The goal is to attain zero drunk driving deaths in Titletown, USA.

The Brown County (Wisconsin) OWI Task Force was launched in 2011. This proactive multiagency approach uses enforcement, education, and awareness to address the drunk driving problem. News media announcements regarding task force locations are made 24 to 48 hours before a deployment, which consists of a large presence of marked squad cars in a concentrated area, typically along routes that drunk drivers are likely to take. The ultimate goal is prevention and to create a perception that if one chooses to drive drunk they will be arrested. A couple of hours into the first Green Bay deployment a taxi cab company called the police department and requested, *"The next time you have a task force deployment, can you please notify us? We can't keep up!"* I thought to myself, "Why can't people be this motivated to get safe rides home all the time?"

Wisconsin is the only state left in the nation where first offense drunk driving is an ordinance violation with no risk of jail time *and* often leads the nation in drunk driving related problems. Binge drinking and intoxication, along with the many societal problems it creates, including drunk driving, is often considered a risky rite of passage. This must change!

Legislators, treatment providers, broadcasters, educational institutions, law enforcement, courts, and corrections must all partner to proactively address the drunk driving problem. Like any type of substance abuse, we must also focus more of our efforts and resources on treating the underlying causes that may attribute to drunk driving arrests.

Until then, more innocent people will continue to suffer needless injuries and death because of drunk driving – The number one preventable crime in America.

Ashley continues to make a difference and I will always share her story to any audience willing to listen.

Ashley's Story – It's why I'm a cop

WWW.ASHLEYSTORY.ORG

DEATH NOTIFICATIONS:

CONCLUDING THOUGHTS

This section is primarily for law enforcement officers, to better educate them about the most difficult assignment they may be asked to carry out – the death notification.

A death notification is a dreaded assignment for law enforcement officers. I have had the chance to ask hundreds of police officers, "If you had to choose between responding to a man with a gun call where your life is potentially at risk OR a death notification, which would you choose?" I have yet to hear a police officer choose the death notification. The primary reason, I have discovered, is because police officers believe they can control the "man with a gun," but they cannot control the response to death.

A proper death notification has an impact on long-term coping. If you have trouble imagining this, that's okay-- I did too until I received Ashley's death notification. I didn't realize the long-term impact of a proper death notification until four years later. I sat down with Brown County Sheriff's Department Deputy Tim Johnson. We met at a restaurant and, for the first time since he notified me of Ashley's death, we talked about it. He started, "Mike, I thought that you would never want to talk to me again, because of what I had to tell you."

I felt horrible that he lived the past four years with that inaccurate perception. Everything that Deputy Johnson did that night was perfect. He conducted the death notification by the book and beyond.

The "Golden Rules" of death notification are:

- In person
- In time
- In pairs
- In plain language
- With compassion

Deputy Johnson followed these principles. He made the notification in person with another deputy, made it as soon as reasonably possible the night of Ashley's death, used very plain language, and with appropriate compassion. Deputy Johnson also went beyond and told me (for the first time five years after Ashley's death), that he had seen our church bulletin on our refrigerator, called our church, and had our pastor respond to the hospital. Our pastor's presence was another small piece that helped us cope in the long term. It may seem odd, but I have nothing but positive memories regarding the way the notification was made. A bad death notification can leave victims with a lifetime of anger and pain.

A death notification should never be made on the phone or any other means of communication. All notifications should be made in person by a minimum of two uniform law enforcement officers. Victim families may experience severe emotional and even physiological reactions to the news. Some may even lash out at the messenger. You must be prepared for any reaction. If available, a member of clergy or crisis counselors can be present to support victims after the notification. It is the duty of the law enforcement officer to make the notification. It is also helpful to have two patrol units available, one to stay with the victim family and another to assist with any transports.

Sadly, too many victim families learn of their loved one's death via social media before a proper death notification can be made. This is yet another reason to make it as soon as possible after death. It is common for victims to disbelieve that a loved one is dead; an in-person notification makes it definitive. This also marks the beginning of healing.

The words used at the time of the notification should be personal, simple, and very clear. Always address the deceased by name versus the impersonal, "the body." Always tell families that their loved one is dead, not that they have "passed on" or "expired." The word *dead* is very definitive and leaves no room for interpretation.

Before knocking on the door, have a plan and know as many details as possible surrounding the victim's death. All information should be shared or obtained by phone, and never over police radio (which can be overheard via police scanners, smart phone applications, or via the Internet). Be prepared to answer the following questions:

- Generally, what were the circumstances surrounding the victim's death?
- Where is the victim at this time?
- Who is the point of contact for additional information?
- Where is the victim's property? Can it be returned or is it evidence?

If you are asked a question that you cannot answer, don't guess or make up a reply. If you don't know the answer to a question, admit that you don't know, but that you will either find out OR provide contact information for the proper authority that can answer it.

As you approach the location of the notification, it's normal to feel stress accompanied by increased heart rate and breathing.

Your stomach may be in knots. Autogenic breathing (slowly inhaling through your nose for four-seconds and then exhaling out your mouth for four-seconds), repeated four times, may help reduce the stress.

Upon knocking and before speaking to the victim family, take a deep breath, and introduce yourself with your name and the agency you represent. Ask to be let inside. At this moment, it is not uncommon for the next of kin to be wary about two law enforcement officers who have unexpectedly shown up at the door; they may ask why. Instead of merely repeating, "Can we please step inside," it's helpful to provide some insight that addresses the "why." One phrase that I have successfully used in these instances is, "I have some very sad news to share with you regarding [name of the deceased] and I would rather sit down and discuss it with you." In all instances, this phrase has allowed me to enter the residence and sit down with the family member. If all reasonable attempts fail, you may be required to make the notification at the front door.

When making the notification, be very clear and use simple, plain language. Speak slowly with an empathetic tone. You may say, "I have some very sad news. I'm sorry to inform you that [name of victim] is dead." Pause and wait for the response-- which may range from disbelief, shock, anger, or rage-- directed at you. I have experienced all of these reactions from next of kin. If you don't know what to say in response to their reaction, you can always safely say, "I'm sorry." It is also acceptable to use the power of touch, such as placing your hand on the person's shoulder, which can be consoling. The victim may also hug or hold onto you. You may also feel an overwhelming sadness, and it's okay to let your emotions show. Of course, being overcome by emotions and unable to function is not acceptable. However, it is better to let a tear roll down your face versus the appearance of indifference. Don't try to talk anyone out of their feelings but rather try to make them feel okay. In reality, there is nothing you can do to make this moment any better. Be mindful not to impose your religious beliefs upon anyone in this situation.

Offer to call a friend or family member to come and be with the next of kin. In cases where there may not be friends or family in the area, make a crisis counselor available to them. Try not to leave a survivor alone.

Be prepared to write down what you tell the next of kin. They will have a difficult time remembering important details, such as answers to the questions mentioned before. Also, be sure to provide them with your business card and any pertinent contact information related to the law enforcement agency handling the investigation, including the report number, phone number, and a primary point of contact.

While the primary officer is making the notification, the other officer can be looking around the immediate area for any helpful information, such as religious affiliation. For example, church bulletins may provide contact information for a priest, pastor, rabbi, or even an imam who can be contacted to respond at the residence or hospital.

In most instances, the survivor will want to view the body of the deceased. It's common for survivors to need to see the deceased with their own eyes to be absolutely convinced their loved ones are dead. Unless there is something that prevents it, such as a body burned beyond recognition or mutilated, plan to transport or make arrangements to have next of kin transported to view the deceased.

Consideration should also be given to providing survivors with information they will need in the next 72-96 hours following the death. Helpful information to provide includes:

- How to obtain death certificates.
- How to obtain a copy of the autopsy results.

- How to obtain copies of police reports.
- Whom to contact related to the investigation or prosecution of the one responsible for causing the death, if applicable.
- How to obtain medical records.
- Crime victim compensation information.
- Notations related to contacting insurance agents and banking institutions.

Some agencies have created survivor information forms, which contain the above-mentioned information, to be left at the notification location.

Take as much time as you need. You will not get a second chance to make the proper death notification. Survivors will forever remember the moment that they were told that their loved one is dead. You want them to remember that you were appropriately caring, empathetic, and helpful during one of the worst moments of their lives.

Here are some true stories of death notifications that were shared by law enforcement officers across the country. Some of these stories will make you laugh. They are not meant to make light of this important duty. Within the humor, valuable lessons can be learned. These stories also demonstrate that anything can happen during a death notification. Expect the unexpected.

The Man in the Wetsuit & Fire Fighter Boots

On one occasion, we responded for a check the welfare. It was a sixty-something year old who had missed two days of work. His vehicle was at the house. We were pretty certain that we would find him dead, which we did. What we did not expect was that he was a fetishist who died in bed wearing a wetsuit and firefighter turnout boots. Search of his residence revealed several other wetsuits, turnout boots, and gas masks. We were not able to find any simple indicators of who to notify. I ended up cold-calling any number I could find scrawled about. (For the youngsters among you, this predated last-number called and other features on today's phones.)

After calling various pizza places and movie theatres, I finally reached a brother-in-law. At this point, there was no reason to be subtle. I simply advised that the decedent had died of apparent natural causes. I later advised the sister after her husband had delivered the news.

The sister called me several days later to thank me for my diplomacy in my notification. She told me that she knew her brother was different, but had thought he was simply gay. She had no idea of his lifestyle. From discussion with the sister, I learned that the decedent had always kept an address book with him (again, before cell phones). We suspect he had brought a lover home and had died during the night. Realizing that he was likely in the date book, we took it and left the residence.

The high point for me was notifying the Homicide Division of the incident, right in the middle of a Washington Redskins game. After describing the scene, I was asked if there were anything unusual about the incident. I don't know, I thought, for all I know we'll flip him over and find a fishing spear in him. In any event, detectives responded to the scene to assist.

Did he Shoot Himself?

I learned to get the facts first hand, if possible. I was dispatched to make a death notification to an ex-wife at a multi-story county executive office building. The husband had died in a suicide. Rather than merely trust second- or third-hand information, I called the agency handling the case. As it turns out, the decedent had been reported as a man with a gun. As officers searched for the suspect, a gunshot was heard. The

110

decedent was found behind a fence, dead of a self-inflicted gun-shot-wound (GSW) to the head. It was unclear if this was a suicide or an accidental GSW while attempting to engage law enforcement.

If you're making a notification for another agency, you will obviously not have all the details. That said, it is important that you be as accurate as possible. It's the mark of a professional and the right thing to do for the family and friends. In this case, simply telling the ex-wife that the decedent was a suicide would have been cruel and could have raised suspicion that law enforcement was covering something up.

In this case, the ex-wife became extremely distraught and refused to believe that the decedent was dead. As requested by the other agency, I attempted to call the investigating officer to put the ex-wife on the phone. In my three decades of calling and being called by the county phone system, I've never know the system to crash. It did that day (this was before cell phones). I ended up bringing the woman to a pay phone in the lobby to call the other agency.

The Right Person for the Job

Though my department has a chaplain service, I have still delivered several death messages in person and was forced to do so by phone also, which I really hated. I suppose I handled them right since I was asked to perform the task over and over. My sergeants have always said I possess the right personality and seemed to know what to say but I never rehearsed anything, I only spoke from the heart but tried to act professional.

My hardest death message was to the parents of a 17-year-old girl that we found (through witnesses) was flirting with a car load of boys as they drove side by side down the road. Though

111

she needed her glasses badly (I found them in her purse), her brother told me she was very self-conscious of how they made her look; so she most likely took them off. She failed to stop for a red light and slammed into a pickup truck and died instantly. She was to graduate high school the very next day. So sad.

My captain called me in to his office back in 1980 and told me, "Your grandfather in Mississippi died of a heart attack." Since he lived in Missouri, I think my reply was, "If he was in Mississippi, he's probably better off, because grandma was gonna kill him anyway, for running off!" I thought it was a bit unprofessional to screw up a death message that bad, so I didn't feel bad about making light of it.

She Was Just at My House

We are a small department of only 8 deputies. One of our deputies happens to be a minister. Any time we have to make a death notification he is called to the scene. This deputy and I make all of the death notifications. I have only been in law enforcement about 3 1/2 years and I have learned that it is not something that you will ever get used to. Telling someone their child or family member won't be coming home. I have learned that you have to have compassion for that family in their time of need.

I will never forget the first death notification I had to make. It was for an 8 year old girl who was riding her bicycle. She lost control, ended up in the middle of a busy street and was struck by an 18-wheeler. He could not stop in time. I had to work the accident and then made the notification. At the time we did not have anyone associated with the ministry to aid in the notification. When I arrived in front of the house and I felt sick to my stomach (I still get that feeling). I approached the house and had to tell the child's mother her baby was not coming home. I will never forget her reaction. It was one of anger and sadness. I guess what made this situation worse for me is this same little girl had just been at my house playing with my daughter the week before. So this hit really close to home. This is one that I will never forget.

Death Notification by Phone

Recently we received a phone call! That's right, a phone call from a medical examiner's office informing us that my wife's brother had committed suicide. Here I work for a sheriff's department that doubles as coroner as well and I'm the assistant chief deputy coroner. They couldn't look at the phone number, area code, or prefix and have one of my deputies make the notification? Plus my wife was the one who answered the phone! Of course they didn't know my line of work, but we NEVER make notifications via phone no matter the circumstances unless we are trying to determine or locate an unknown next of kin.

I'm Sorry, Officer

About 8 years ago I responded to a fatal crash and when I got there I found a 16-year-old boy under the medic's blanket. He looked so peaceful, like he was sleeping. He had no outward trauma, it was all internal. I made the notification and took a department chaplain with me. I can only imagine what the father thought when he saw a police officer and priest at his door at 2:00 a.m. He looked at us as he opened the door and did nothing but back up from the door as we entered and never said a word. The kid's last name was a Polish name and I was a bit afraid I'd mispronounce it. The father was a big strong man and I could tell he was tough just by looking at him. After I gave him the news he dropped to the floor and cried out loud like a baby. I am certain I am but a handful of people in his life who have ever seen him cry. He called his ex-wife and she later told me she wasn't sure if he was serious or not. She showed up at his house and later told me she knew it was serious because she saw the pain in my eyes. She actually told me later she felt sorry for ME! I have remained friends with both of them. It was one of the hardest notifications I have ever made.

Man Reported Dead Walks in Front Door

I worked a case that involved a 20-year-old who died in a motorcycle crash. I retrieved his I.D. from his wallet and we all thought he looked taller than the I.D. card indicated, but didn't think much more of it. I went and made the notification and left after a time. I was back at the station typing when the radio room supervisor called me and told me the family I had just left called to tell me their son had just walked in the door. I was dumbfounded because the picture on the I.D. WAS the deceased. I went back to the house and sure enough the son was there, but not the same person who was on the I.D. I showed him the I.D. and asked if he knew the person in the picture. He told me it was his friend who was under 20 and must have used his I.D. to get one under his friend's name so he could go out to bars and drink. I asked the 21-year-old if he had any idea how his friend got his information in order to get an I.D. card and he only said, "He must have taken it." I chewed on him for a bit to tell him I put his parents through hell by telling them he was dead. I then left and had to make another notification of the correct family and explained to them why it took so long for the notification. It's hard enough having to do the notification, but to have to tell the parents their son had a fake I.D. makes it that much harder.

He's Got a Gun!

Fortunately on this night, I had a ride-along with me from another jurisdiction and at about 1:30 a.m., we were dispatched to meet with the assistant coroner and one of the chaplains on a darkened dirt road. The two-car fatality we were on-scene with only a few hours earlier that evening (and less than mile away) had a drunk driver killing a sweet 80+ year old lady on her way home. Her son supposedly lived in a trailer somewhere in the general vicinity of her little house on that dirt road, but the two ladies from coroner's and chaplain's offices said they only had a general idea, but were unsure of the address, as no phone number could be located. We finally found the right dilapidated old trailer, with a light inside and a yapping dog out back. After ten minutes of knocking on the door, nobody answered. The ride-along and I walked back up the path to the dirt roadway where the ladies were waiting by their vehicles. I decided to knock on the door of a crappy wooden shack next door, which looked like it had caught fire on more than one occasion, had sunk into the earth in several spots, and was breaking apart. I didn't expect to find anybody inside and at least I could say we tried everywhere on the property.

To our surprise, the old door opened up and our flashlights revealed a completely naked and intoxicated male subject in his late 40's, pointing a shotgun right at my waist (with no affordable cover nearby for me). Of course our Glock and Sig Sauer 40's came out of their respective holsters in a heartbeat. Thankfully we were able to convince him we were legit and not looking to rob him. After multiple commands of, "*Put the gun down!*" he finally complied. I had to climb into that creature-infested shack to recover the shotgun (which was not loaded, though it wouldn't have mattered seconds earlier) and verify that the guy could maneuver the burnt-out mattress and neck-high pile of refuse inside to put on something decent, before escorting him back outside so we could meet with the ladies.

Due to his drunken state, he didn't believe them when they told him about his mother's death. He was still in disbelief when we cleared the scene 15mins later. My ride-along and I drove off with the usual, "Holy Shit!" comments to each other on how BADLY that call could have turned out.

115

You usually expect it to, "hit the fan" AFTER you've made the notification, not when you first get there. I was definitely thankful I had an armed ride-along with me that night, just in case it had gone even further downhill, although it would have been a cluster getting my ride-along involved in an on-duty shooting.

No He's Not!

I was dispatched to a check the welfare call at an apartment that I had been sent to multiple times. The 20-year-old guy [we will call him Mike] that lived there was the often drunk "apartment manager" and son of the complex owner. All three of us knew each other on a first name basis.

The deceased had a two-year old daughter, but had a strained relationship with the mother. She had come over and believed he was dead, but was afraid to check. The apartment door was open when I arrived and she was frantic. I found him on his back on top of a weight bench. He had put 135 pounds on bench press bar and dropped it on his throat. He left a note indicating his intent. It has been the most unique way that I have seen somebody kill themselves. Myself and another officer lifted the barbell of his throat and a rush of air exhaled from him. The odor was overpowering; the odor of death.

Since I knew his father, I was logically the one that would make the notification. I called his father and asked him to come over to the apartment complex. I don't recall what I told him, but I didn't make the notification on the phone. He arrived a few minutes later. I met him outside the complex at the main entrance. I simply told him, "I'm sorry, I have some bad news to tell you, but Mike is dead." He screamed, "No he's not!" and at the same time grabbed me with both his hands by my chest and shoulders and shoved me into the brick wall. I placed both my hands on top of his, looked him right in the eye, and said, "I'm sorry." He let go of me and just

116

sobbed. He was allowed to see Mike and I think that was the right decision. Although we believed it was a suicide, we treated it like a homicide scene and had it secured. I helped him make funeral home arrangements and he was later able to see Mike at the hospital.

No...That's Not Him!

I was a road supervisor and one of my primary duties was to make or assist with making death notifications. We had received a request from another agency to notify the owner of a vehicle that the driver, believed to be her boyfriend, had been killed. He had tried to pass another vehicle on country road and collided head on with a semi-tractor and trailer. Myself and another uniform patrol officer went to the owner's listed address and she didn't live there anymore. The patrol officer went back in-service, but I was determined to find the vehicle owner. I ultimately located a phone number for her and obtained her current address. She was suspicious of my phone call and asked why I had to meet her in person. I told her that her vehicle had been involved in a crash and I needed to speak with her about the driver. I didn't tell her that he was dead.

I arrived at her address alone because no other officers were available. She met me outside on the sidewalk. It was evident that she knew something was wrong. I asked her if we could go inside and talk and she refused. I asked her if we could then sit on the porch and talk and she again refused. She demanded to know what was wrong. I told her, "I'm sorry to tell you that your boyfriend is dead." At that moment, I had forgotten his name. She collapsed into my arms and cried. Her tears ran down and dripped off my badge. While holding her with my right hand, I opened my notebook with my left and I said, "I just want to make sure that your boyfriend is..." and I said the name that the other agency had given me. She lifted her head off of my shoulder and said, "No, that's not him."

I felt horrible, embarrassed, and angry. "How the hell could the coroner screw this up," I thought. I told her that there must be a mistake and asked her again if we could go inside so I could make some phone calls. I followed her inside and reached the coroner on my cell phone. I told him what happened and clearly said, "Are you sure it is…" and repeated the name they gave me. He assured me that was his name. I asked him if the deceased had any tattoos or other identifiers. As he described the tattoos to me and I repeated them back while writing them in my notebook, she began to cry again. I ended the phone call and she then told me his real name.

It turns out that her boyfriend was in fact dead. However, this was her "new" boyfriend that had found and taken her "old" boyfriends identification card that he had left behind. Ironically, they looked rather similar in life and in death.

Although this was a unique notification, it reinforced the importance of ensuring that you have the correct information before making the notification.

Concluding Thoughts about Death Notification

The difficult task of a death notification can carried out with necessary empathy and professionalism by applying the following:

- Have another officer with you. If possible, bring a victim advocate, Chaplin, or crisis counselor along.

- Be direct. Tell the loved ones you have bad news, then tell them the bad news. Be blunt: their relative has died, is dead, has been killed; not passed on, not passed away, not gone to a better place. You may understand those vague terms. The people you're notifying may not. Death is definitive and the words you use must not leave room for error or misinterpretation.

- Give the family a contact number at the hospital, including how to reach the medical examiner's office, homicide unit, or wherever and whomever they need to call for more information. Try to leave them in the company of a friend or loved one. Never leave the grieving survivors alone.

A death notification is obviously an emotionally impacting moment for the recipients, but also for the officers. When the officers walk away from the notification, the impression they left upon the grieving families will be remembered. Similarly, the impression upon the officers will be everlasting and we must ensure that we are emotionally and psychologically okay as well. Don't be afraid to reach out for help, not only with these emotionally difficult assignments, but in all aspects of your work. Failing to take care of our emotional and psychological wellbeing can lead to our demise, and that is not acceptable.

RESOURCES

Ashley's Story, http://www.ashleystory.org/

Bennett, Thomas, L. "In Person, In Time" – Procedures for Death Notification. Accessed July 20, 2015. http://www.nationalcops.org/downloads/in_person.pdf

Bureau of Justice Statistics - Alcohol and Violent Crime in the U.S.: Table 31. Alcohol use at the time of offense by state and federal prisoners, by type of offense, 2004. (2010, July 28). Retrieved January 10, 2016, from http://www.bjs.gov/content/acf/29_prisoners_and_alcoholu se.cfm

Concerns of Police Survivors, http://www.nationalcops.org/

Green Bay Family Fun Run, http://www.familyfunrun.org/

Mothers Against Drunk Driving, http://www.madd.org/

87564852R00070

Made in the USA
Lexington, KY
26 April 2018